A Gestalt Approach to Couples Therapy

This book offers a framework for understanding and improving relationships through the lens of Gestalt therapy. It examines the paradox of intimacy—how genuine connection emerges from embracing individuality in a relationship—and how to navigate the dynamic tension between autonomy and togetherness.

Readers will benefit from practical tools, theoretical insights, and engaging case examples designed to deepen their understanding of relationship dynamics. Therapists will find innovative strategies to foster presence, differentiation, and creative transformation in their clients. Couples can uncover ways to turn conflict into connection, discovering how their differences can energize and strengthen their relationships. The book's unique integration of Gestalt therapy principles with cross-cultural perspectives makes it particularly relevant for navigating the complexities of modern relationships. With its theoretical rigor and practical applications, the book bridges the gap between research and clinical practice, offering fresh insights into the evolving field of couples therapy. By addressing pressing post-pandemic relational challenges and integrating diverse cultural perspectives, it provides a transformative guide for those engaged in understanding and fostering human connection. This approach enables readers to be able to reframe differences as opportunities for growth rather than sources of conflict.

This text is an essential resource for academics, researchers, and students interested in relationship science and therapeutic approaches. It is especially relevant for mental health professionals, including practicing therapists, counsellors, and social workers, as well as those in training programs.

Nicole Chew-Helbig, PhD, is a certified Integrative Gestalt psychotherapist and counsellor based in Singapore. She holds a doctorate in psychotherapy science from Sigmund Freud University, Vienna. She is a member of the Singapore Association of Counselling, and the Singapore Psychological Society.

A Gestalt Approach to Couples Therapy

The Dance of Difference

Nicole Chew-Helbig

Routledge
Taylor & Francis Group
LONDON AND NEW YORK

Designed cover image: smodj

First published 2026
by Routledge
4 Park Square, Milton Park, Abingdon, Oxon OX14 4RN

and by Routledge
605 Third Avenue, New York, NY 10158

Routledge is an imprint of the Taylor & Francis Group, an informa business

British Library Cataloguing-in-Publication Data
A catalogue record for this book is available from the British Library

ISBN: 978-1-041-05148-0 (hbk)
ISBN: 978-1-041-05146-6 (pbk)
ISBN: 978-1-003-63154-5 (ebk)

DOI: 10.4324/9781003631545

Typeset in Galliard
by SPi Technologies India Pvt Ltd (Straive)

Contents

Illustrations

Figure

Tables

Preface

Looking back on my journey into couples therapy, I recall a turning point in Ljubljana, Slovenia, during the summer of 2015. My husband, Oliver, and I volunteered to be a "model couple" for a Gestalt Associates Training Los Angeles (GATLA) European summer residential. We had no idea what to expect. The room was large and elegantly carpeted, with bright lights that matched the energy of our assembled group. Bob was recording, as he often did during these summer residential sessions, capturing every moment of the therapeutic process.

Oliver and I sat opposite each other in simple chairs, while Bob and his wife, Rita, sat beside us, forming an X shape. The atmosphere was electric with potential. At the time, I was a newly qualified Gestalt therapist, having travelled from Carinthia, Austria, where we lived, just a two-hour drive through the Karawanks mountain range. As our final session drew to a close, I recall the intense silence that filled the room. My gaze moved from Rita to Bob, then to Oliver, and back to Bob. The shared connection between our eyes, hearts, and breath felt tangible.

"The room is silent," Bob said softly, "this is the feeling of Grace."

His words sank deep, imprinting themselves on my memory and being. It wasn't just an abstract idea, but a lived experience of what happens when we're truly seen in relationship. For Oliver and me, this became a guiding principle—what it means to meet each other authentically, even in the presence of others who had been strangers just a week earlier. I'm profoundly thankful to Bob, who has since passed away, and Rita. Their presence transformed something essential in how I understand relationship work.

Since that experience, I've found myself returning to two persistent questions: Why do so many couples struggle to find true intimacy despite their best efforts? How do the differences that initially attract us often become sources of conflict? These questions have no simple answers, but they deserve exploration.

Conventional approaches to couples therapy, including Emotionally Focused Therapy (EFT) and the Gottman Method (Gottman & Gottman, 2015), emphasise communication skills, conflict resolution, and emotional bonding through the lens of attachment theory. EFT, for instance, seeks to rebuild emotional connection by fostering secure attachment and helping partners express unmet emotional needs (Johnson & Sims, 2001), while also improving attachment security and relationship satisfaction. Similarly, the Gottman Method focuses on emotional attunement, regulating conflict, and fostering mutual understanding, showing strong results in reducing emotional divorce and enhancing communication patterns. The approach discussed in this book complements and extends beyond the couples therapist's work, not by introducing additional techniques, but by centring the therapeutic focus on the relationship field and acknowledging the unique individual differences within the couple. Isn't this what couples usually come to therapy for? To reconnect. However, the reconnection need not come at the expense of their individuality.

Differences connect and grate. Contrary to the conventional tendency to address differences by attempting to make them disappear, the work presented in this book elaborates on the notion that healing in relationships occurs when these differences are fully acknowledged, honoured, and accepted. The ongoing debate between attachment and differentiation theories reflects this tension: while attachment theory focuses on emotional closeness, differentiation theory argues that intimacy flourishes when two well-defined, autonomous individuals engage each other fully (Hardy & Fisher, 2018). Therefore, while conventional models offer tools for relational repair, they may overlook the more profound truth that intimacy thrives on connection and the presence of two distinct selves.

I observed that couples who tried hardest to eliminate their differences often struggled the most. One partner might suppress their needs to maintain harmony, while another might demand change to create sameness. Yet the couples who found genuine intimacy learned to dance with their differences rather than fight against them. This aspect of the Gestalt therapeutic practice offers a unique lens for understanding this dance (Resnick, 2020). Rather than seeing relationship problems as skills deficits or communication failures, it recognises them as creative adaptations within a complex field of forces. Through concepts like contact boundaries, field theory, and phenomenological awareness, Gestalt therapy illuminates how partners can meet authentically at the boundary of their differences.

I do not position Gestalt couples therapy as superior to other modalities or as a replacement for other concepts, but believe that all modalities belong in the field; it is not an "either–or" but an "and." While other schools have sought to brand themselves, Gestalt is not a brand but a historically significant development in psychotherapy that arose from psychoanalysis with Fritz and Lore Perls, together with Hefferline and Goodman (Bocian, 2010). The theoretical understanding presented here is crucial to the effectiveness of therapy. Yet, it has sometimes been lost in other modalities because Gestalt therapy's essence lies in contact and field phenomena.

The stories on these pages are creative non-fiction and composed of composite characters and scenes. As autoethnographers can explain, storytelling is the best way to present qualitative empirical evidence. It is also transformative for the reader, which is my aim. Storytelling is how traditional healers and psychotherapists learn best from our mentors. This book is written to be smooth to read, and it has stretched my capabilities as a writer. I am, after all, a practitioner first.

The stories you'll encounter are composites drawn from hours of clinical experience. While the specific details have been altered to protect confidentiality, the emotional truth of each narrative remains intact. Through these stories, you'll witness how couples navigate the complex terrain of intimacy, cultural introjects, trauma, and separation.

Who This Book Is For

A Gestalt Approach to Couples Therapy: The Dance of Difference speaks to several audiences, each of whom will find unique value in its pages.

For couples therapists and counsellors, this book offers a fresh perspective on working with relationship dynamics. Whether you're already familiar with Gestalt therapy or come from another theoretical orientation, you'll find practical insights for the work. The phenomenological approach, field theory, and creative experimentation detailed here will enrich your therapeutic toolkit, offering alternatives to techniques that may have reached their limits.

This book provides a comprehensive introduction to approaching relationship issues from a Gestalt perspective for individual therapists looking to expand into couples work. Rather than presenting formulas or protocols, it shows how to work with what emerges in the room, trusting the wisdom of the therapeutic field.

For students of psychology and counselling, this book bridges theory and practice, showing how philosophical concepts like phenomenology, field theory, and dialogue feature in therapeutic work. The case studies provide windows into the therapeutic process that textbooks alone cannot offer.

A Note on Cultural Representation

This book emerges from therapeutic work in Singapore's multicultural context, viewed through my lens as a therapist trained in Western modalities. I don't claim to represent any culture authentically—that's impossible for anyone to do, as cultures are living, diverse, and constantly evolving.

The couples presented here are creative composites designed to illustrate therapeutic principles, not cultural realities. Where cultural details appear, they serve the therapeutic narrative rather than anthropological accuracy. I've deliberately chosen scenarios that could occur across multiple cultural contexts while acknowledging that culture shapes every aspect of human relationships.

In the therapy room, clients sometimes articulate culturally inappropriate, internally racist, or misogynistic remarks. I have included such moments in these stories not because I endorse these views, but because this is what happens in real therapy. These expressions often represent cultural introjects—beliefs swallowed whole from family and society—that clients are in the process of examining. Through the therapeutic process, people learn to differentiate between inherited beliefs and their own authentic values, keeping what serves them while releasing what constrains. The brief responses and contextualisations I provide in each chapter aim to show this process of examination without judgement.

It's worth noting that readers of this English-language book are likely influenced by Western perspectives to some degree, potentially sharing similar cultural lenses. This shared framework may make certain dynamics more immediately recognisable while others remain less visible. I encourage all readers to remain curious about their own cultural assumptions as they engage with these stories.

Cultural details appear when therapeutically significant–When Mei talks about being the eldest in a Chinese family, or when Markus from Germany voices out his expectations, these details are significant because they influence the therapeutic encounter. This does not mean that everyone in this culture responds in the same way as in the story. It also does not suggest that similar situations never occur in other cultures.

Individuals transcend categories–My experience practising in Singapore has taught me that individuals are inherently unique. While cultural influences certainly shape us, no person can be solely defined by their race, religion, or cultural background. The businessman who seems traditionally Western may hold deep collective values; the seemingly conservative local family might embrace progressive ideals. We are all more complex than the labels we are given.

Avoiding cultural stereotypes–I urge readers not to use these fictional clients to draw conclusions about any specific culture or people. I created them for illustrative purposes only! Siya's struggle with family expectations reveals something about Siya, not about all women from her cultural background. Sam's relationship with his mother reflects their unique dynamic, not universal patterns across any community.

The universality within specificity–While each couple's story emerges from particular cultural contexts, the themes explored–the longing for connection, the fear of difference, the weight of shame, the dance between intimacy and autonomy–transcend cultural boundaries. These are human struggles, dressed in different cultural clothing but sharing a common essence.

In our increasingly interconnected world, most of us carry multiple cultural influences. These complex identities resist over-simplified categorisation.

A Note on Socioeconomic Context

The client stories in this book primarily feature individuals from middle-class backgrounds. This reflects both the scope of the book and the reality that relationship dynamics manifest differently across socioeconomic contexts. While the fundamental principles of Gestalt therapy apply universally, economic stress, systemic inequalities, and limited access to resources create additional layers of complexity that deserve their own dedicated exploration.

Rather than attempting to address all contexts superficially, I've chosen to focus on relationship patterns that emerge when basic material needs are relatively stable. This allows us to examine personality differences, cultural influences, and relational dynamics with clarity. In practice, most clients' lives are far more complex than these illustrative cases suggest—real therapeutic work always involves multiple intersecting challenges.

I sincerely recognise that relationship struggles in communities facing economic and security hardship often involve additional pressures: financial stress, limited privacy, fewer choices, and systemic barriers to well-being. These contexts require not just therapeutic insight but also acknowledgement of material realities and structural change. While beyond this book's scope, such work is equally vital and deserves its own comprehensive treatment.

I hope that by clearly delineating what this book addresses—and what it doesn't—readers can apply these insights appropriately within their own contexts while recognising where additional considerations may be needed.

The therapeutic principles explored in this book—attending to difference, working with what emerges, honouring individual wholeness within relationship—remain relevant across all socioeconomic contexts, and their application must be thoughtfully adapted. My intention is not to suggest that relationship work happens in isolation from material conditions, but rather to offer one piece of a larger conversation about how we meet each other across difference. I trust readers to discern how these insights might serve their own work and lives, whether in private practice rooms or community settings, whether addressing relationship dynamics alone or as part of broader systemic interventions. The dance of difference continues wherever two people attempt genuine meeting, and that dance deserves our careful attention regardless of the stage on which it unfolds.

References

Bocian, B. (2010). *Fritz Perls in Berlin 1893–1933: Expressionism, psychoanalysis, Judaism*. EHP Verlag.

Gottman, J. M. & Gottman, J. S. (2015). *The seven principles for making marriage work*. Harmony Books.

Hardy, N. M. & Fisher, A. R. (2018). Attachment versus differentiation: The contemporary couple therapy debate. *Family Process*, 57(2), 557–571.

Johnson, S. M. & Sims, A. (2001). The work of emotionally focused therapy with couples. In *Clinical handbook of couple therapy* (3rd ed., pp. 91–110). Guilford Press.

Resnick, R. W. (2020). *A couple of individuals: Introduction to Gestalt therapy [Video]*. YouTube. https://www.youtube.com/watch?v=gXG8DOtmmlk&t

About the Author

Nicole Chew-Helbig, PhD, is a Singapore-born psychotherapist and researcher whose work brings Gestalt therapy into dialogue with Asian cultural experience. Trained in both the European and American streams of Gestalt thought, her clinical and academic work is grounded in phenomenology, embodied presence, and field theory.

Her research explores how cultural, relational, and bodily processes shape the therapeutic moment. Through autoethnographic and field-theoretical inquiry, she investigates how intergenerational histories, social forces, and atmospheric qualities of the field influence what emerges between people.

Working in Singapore—a confluence of ancestral, linguistic, and relational traditions—her practice centres on clients and couples navigating cultural differences, inherited patterns, and the paradoxes of intimacy. Her scholarship aims to articulate an Asian-inflected understanding of Gestalt therapy that honours lived experience and local wisdom.

Outside her clinical and research life, Nicole writes and reflects in the quiet company of her husband of more than two decades, Oliver, and their dog, whose steady presence reminds her that genuine contact—like art—arises where technique meets responsiveness and the courage to stay with what unfolds.

Introduction

The Dance of Difference

> "Love is an active power in man; a power which breaks through the walls which separate man from his fellow men, which unites him with others; love makes him overcome the sense of isolation and separateness, yet it permits him to be himself, to retain his integrity. In love, the paradox occurs that two beings become one and yet remain two."
>
> Erich Fromm (1956, p. 20)

When Two Become None

"And the two shall become one flesh." This historical vision of marriage has shaped relationships for millennia, promising unity, stability, and belonging. Yet hidden within this promise lies a paradox that haunts modern couples: when two truly become one, there's none (Resnick, 2020).

Picture placing your hand in water perfectly matched to your body temperature. The boundary where skin meets water—that vital edge where sensation occurs—simply disappears. Without difference, there's no contact. Without contact, there's no genuine connection. Like that hand in temperature-matched water, couples who achieve perfect unity often find themselves unable to feel each other at all.

This fusion model of relationships emerged when survival depended on clearly defined roles and economic interdependence. In traditional societies, whether Western or Eastern, marriage served primarily social and economic functions rather than emotional fulfilment. Partners knew their place, their duties, and their expectations. The model worked—not because it created happiness, but because it ensured survival.

Today, this template poorly serves couples seeking both connection and individuality. Modern relationships must navigate unprecedented challenges: geographic mobility that separates us from extended family support, dual careers that strain traditional arrangements, and the expectation that one person should fulfil virtually all our emotional, social, and practical needs. The nuclear family, isolated from broader community networks, places demands on couples that no single relationship can sustainably bear.

DOI: 10.4324/9781003631545-1

The consequences are visible everywhere. Beyond the well-documented divorce rates, there exists what Bob Resnick (2020) calls the "secretly miserably married"—couples enduring unfulfilling relationships out of fear, financial dependency, social pressure, or concern for children. Even more telling is the growing number who choose to remain single, viewing partnership itself as too threatening an endeavour. The fusion model, rather than creating lasting bonds, often drives people away from intimate connection altogether.

The Paradox of Attraction and Threat

Here lies the central paradox of intimate relationships: the very differences that initially attract us—what some call the "spark of otherness"—later become sources of conflict and threat. In the early stages of romance, we're drawn to partners who embody qualities we lack or admire. Their differentness excites us, expands our world, makes us feel more alive.

Yet as relationships deepen, psychological forces drive us toward sameness. This isn't merely personal preference but a deeply embedded protective mechanism. Throughout human history, difference has signaled potential danger—the stranger, the outsider, the other who might threaten our survival. These patterns, while adaptive in their original context, now sabotage our most intimate connections.

Watch any couple in conflict, and you'll likely witness one of three predictable responses to difference:

1. **Deferring**: One partner chronically gives in. "Yes, dear" becomes their refrain, creating temporary harmony at devastating cost. As Resnick notes, "I lose me. I'm not there representing my truth, who I am, my needs." The very self that could participate in genuine connection gradually disappears.
2. **Withdrawing**: Partners pull away to avoid confronting differences. They craft parallel lives, carefully choreographed to minimise contact. This avoids conflict but creates a different loss: "I lose the other. I lose connection." The relationship becomes a shell, maintaining form while lacking substance.
3. **Changing the Other**: The most damaging response attempts to eliminate difference by reshaping the partner. This defines conflict itself—difference becomes conflict when one tries to change the other to be more like oneself. The escalation that follows often mirrors geopolitical strife, with each side trying to impose its values on the other.

None of these strategies work because they misidentify the problem. Difference itself isn't the enemy—our response to it is.

The Connection Model: A Radical Reframe

The Gestalt perspective fundamentally redefines understanding: difference is not merely something to accept in relationships but is actually crucial. This idea challenges long-held beliefs about love, marriage, and intimacy, replacing them with what Resnick (2020) calls the "connection model." According to this model, contact—the key element of meaningful relationships—happens precisely at the point where partners experience their differences. Just as we can't feel water that matches our body temperature, we can't truly sense another person without the boundary of difference. This boundary both separates and links, creating the conditions necessary for authentic connection.

While "contact" describes specific moments of encounter at the boundary, "connection" encompasses the entire flow of dance—the rhythm of approaching and withdrawing, touching and parting. Healthy relationships require this dynamic movement.

The therapist's role isn't to choreograph this dance, but to become integral to the couple's lived environment where their dance takes place.

Who You'll Meet in this Book

The pages ahead contain nine couples' stories, each arriving in therapy with what seems like a straightforward problem—communication breakdowns, intimacy barriers, cultural conflicts. Yet as their sessions unfold, deeper patterns emerge. A wife's exhaustion reveals decades of caretaking. A husband's drinking masks the terror of abandonment. What appears as withdrawal is protection; what looks like intrusion is a desperate need for connection.

These are composite stories of real and fictional characters, crafted from clinical experience to illustrate concepts and atmospheric effects and provide an interesting read. While the characters are not real people, you may, for example, recognise yourself in Sarah's careful distance or Liam's vigilant anxiety. You might also see your relationship reflected in Emma and James's parallel lives or Mei and Markus's cultural negotiations. Even the metaphorical couple—Cinderella and her Prince discovering that "happily ever after" is where real struggle begins—may feel unexpectedly familiar to many.

Each couple illuminates a different facet of Gestalt therapy's approach to relationships. Through their journeys, you'll discover how staying present with immediate experience, rather than rushing toward solutions, creates space for genuine transformation.

Each chapter is crafted to immerse you in the lived experience of therapy, demonstrating how transformation emerges from presence rather than procedure.

Table 0.1 Who You'll Meet in This Book

Couple	*Presenting Issue*	*Gestalt Theme*
Sarah & John	Decades of careful distance	Phenomenological witnessing
Liam & Akina	His drinking, her withdrawal	Trauma as creative adjustment
Mei & Markus	Cultural differences, unspoken grief	Paradoxical theory of change
Sherlyn & Derrick	Three years without intimacy	Invisible audiences
Hai & David	Intellectual connection masking distance	Embodied experiments
Emma & James	Living as strangers in same home	Wordless connection
Siya & Sam	Addiction and cultural expectations	Field forces
Liza & Claudia	Hidden same-sex relationship	Shame as field phenomenon
Ben & Jenn	Betrayal and shattered trust	Creative indifference
Cinderella & Prince	After "happily ever after"	When fairy tales meet reality

The book is organized into four main parts:

- **Part I: Foundations of Presence** introduces the phenomenological approach and how trauma manifests in relationships.
- **Part II: The Paradox of Change** explores the paradoxical theory of change and experimental work.
- **Part III: The Field and Connection** examines field theory, cultural shame, and the contact cycle.
- **Part IV: Integration and Practice** covers creative indifference, integration with other modalities, and clinical applications.

Throughout these stories, you'll witness how lasting change emerges not from eliminating differences but from developing what Fritz Perls called "response-ability"—the capacity to respond flexibly rather than from habitual patterns. This involves becoming curious about differences rather than threatened by them, exploring their meaning rather than trying to erase them.

An Invitation to Dance

As you read these pages, you're invited not just to learn about Gestalt couples therapy but to experience it. Notice your own responses to these couples' struggles. Feel how their patterns might echo in your own relationships. Allow yourself to be touched by their courage to stay present with difficulty rather than fleeing into easy answers.

This book doesn't promise to solve relationship problems or eliminate conflict. Instead, it offers something more valuable: a way of being with difference that transforms it from a threat to a gift. When couples learn to dance with their differences rather than despite them, they discover what Erich Fromm called love's essential paradox—two beings becoming one while remaining two.

In our increasingly polarised world, this capacity to hold difference without eliminating it offers hope beyond the therapy room. The principles explored here—staying present with what is, maintaining a presence between polarities, trusting the wisdom of the field—apply wherever differences create both challenge and possibility.

The dance of difference awaits. Will you join?

References

Fromm, E. (1956). *The art of loving*. Harper & Row.

Resnick, R. W. (2020). *A couple of individuals: Introduction to Gestalt therapy [Video]*. Youtube. https://www.youtube.com/watch?v=gXG8DOtmmlk&t

Part I

Foundations of Presence

1 First Contact

The Phenomenological Encounter

"Feeling cared for is foreign to me."

—Sarah

The Phenomenological Foundation of Gestalt Couples Therapy

When couples enter the therapy room, they bring more than their stories and struggles—they create an immediate, living reality that speaks before words are uttered. The phenomenological approach in Gestalt therapy offers a radical way of meeting this reality: not through analysis or interpretation, but through direct, embodied awareness of what is happening in the here-and-now.

This approach draws from Husserl's (1913) phenomenological method, particularly the practice of bracketing or epoché. In Gestalt therapy, bracketing doesn't mean complete detachment from our knowledge and experience. It involves maintaining dual awareness: we remain conscious of our assumptions, theoretical frameworks, and personal biases while intentionally setting them aside to perceive with fresh openness. Like placing parentheses around our habitual ways of knowing, we acknowledge their presence without allowing them to direct the therapeutic encounter.

The here-and-now experience forms the cornerstone of this approach (Perls, Hefferline & Goodman, 1951; Stern, 2004). Rather than excavating the past or planning the future, we prioritise the immediate reality unfolding between people. This focus brings the therapeutic process into contact through presence between the therapist and the clients. When we attune to this atmospheric dimension, we move beyond diagnosing individual pathology to sensing the living field of the relationship itself.

Perhaps most distinctive to Gestalt therapy is its emphasis on pre-verbal, pre-reflexive awareness. This level of consciousness operates before language intervenes, before our minds categorise and label. It's the immediate bodily knowing that arises when someone enters a room—that instant sense of heaviness or lightness, expansion or contraction. Rather than quickly naming these experiences ("you seem anxious"), we stay with the phenomenon itself ("I notice your shoulders lifting toward your ears").

DOI: 10.4324/9781003631545-3

This pre-reflexive awareness requires the willingness to be uncertain (Staemmler, 2009). Instead of rushing to understand or interpret, the phenomenological therapist cultivates radical openness to whatever emerges. We become witnesses to the couple's dance, attending to the subtle choreography of approach and withdrawal, the quality of silence between words, the way bodies orient toward or away from each other.

In couples therapy, this phenomenological stance transforms how we understand problems. Rather than viewing issues as residing within individuals—one partner's "communication problem" or another's "intimacy issues"—we perceive how patterns emerge from the space between people. The therapist does not observe from outside but actively engages in the therapeutic process, participating through their own sensations, impulses, and responses, providing valuable insights into the couple's world.

What follows is a couple's story, illustrating how these phenomenological principles are enacted in real life. As you read about Sarah and John, observe how their entire relationship unfolds through immediate phenomena—such as a chair turning slightly away, fingers entwined in anticipation, or the presence filling the room before any words are spoken. This exemplifies phenomenology in action: the daring act of perceiving what is, before our theories shape its interpretation.

Sarah and John

John perches stiffly on the sofa's edge, his fingers knotted. His short grey beard frames a face tanned from toiling on the golf course. Though his batik shirt offers a splash of life, it seems out of place against his subdued form.

Sarah adjusts the angle of the swivel chair. Her beige linen shift dress is a muted statement of modest elegance. Her posture reminds me of a guard. She leans on an armrest, creating just enough distance to suggest a retreat. The corners of her mouth tighten.

Silence pools between us.

When she finally breaks the silence, her voice strikes a discordant note. "There are so many things wrong," she says, "I don't even know where to start."

"And yet, you've just started," I say, leaning in.

A smile flickers across her face, dying before it reaches her eyes. She turns the chair, angling it slightly away from us.

John's shoulders are hunched forward, reminiscent of a schoolboy waiting for a lesson to begin. He nods and waits. This is his first time in a therapy room. "I'm a practical man," he says firmly. I'm here to help do whatever needs doing."

Sarah cuts in, "I feel like I'm walking on eggshells because anytime a bomb will be detonated." She shifts in her chair, creaking it, her fingers drumming on the armrest. Not waiting for our responses, she breaks into a litany of her life, of their daughters—Clarissa's new job, Vanessa's university housing search, and Alyssa's IB exams—her words rolling into the space between us.

"I notice a change in your facial expression as you speak of your girls," I note, to which she didn't comment. Sarah's words—"a bomb will be detonated"—hang heavy between us. I glance at John, who remains still. My mind drifts, sensing a weightiness in the room. I pull myself back, refocusing on Sarah. "I envision what a detonation might look like here," I say.

"Recently, we have stopped talking altogether," Sarah lets her voice drop off.

John adjusts his spine upright and focuses on me. I instinctively acknowledge his attention with a nod.

"I would do my things, and she would defer to the girls," he says, clearing his throat, "When she gets upset..."

"You just watch TV. It's that easy for you," Sarah's words slicing through the air before John could finish.

"What would you rather John do?" I ask.

"I don't know. I'd rather have a combat." Sarah shoots back.

"I want to be easy-going, but it has become so black and white with us." John mutters.

"So when things feel black-and-white, it's hard to be easy-going?" I check.

"I get frustrated, and then I can't control it."

I absently pick up a bright pink plastic stress ball on my coffee table, its spiky tips glimmering in the light. The spikes against my palm offer me some solace. I hand it to John.

John accepts the ball and glides his fingers over its rough surface. His downcast eyes make him seem reflective. "I try to downplay it," he says.

"I'm tired of trying." Sarah's words hung before I could ask John what "it" meant.

"I want to do the right thing," John says, gazing at the ball in his hand. "I try to anticipate what to do so as not to rile her up, and I am lost."

"I feel misunderstood." Sarah's voice cracks. "I just want you to get me, for once."

I hold back my impulse to respond to Sarah, curious about the possibility of momentarily interrupting her push for space.

I lean back in my seat, saying instead to John, "What if, for a brief moment, we allow ourselves to be easy-going? Do you know how to do that?"

A quick smile flashes across his face. "I have forgotten how it feels. I used to be described as easy-going in my school days. My childhood was carefree."

"I guess you remember a little of that feeling."

John lets himself sink back into the sofa. Fiddling with the spiky plastic object, a change crosses his face. His eyes soften. The room falls silent.

Sarah shifts in the chair. Her gaze sharpens at John. She lets out a breath. "I feel bad," she lets out a breath, "Like responsible."

"I wonder what it would sound like if you told John what you are responsible for," I say.

"Dragging you here, John. To therapy." She looks at him. He doesn't look up.

"And now, John is easy-going, and you're responsible," I say. I invite her to notice what she's sensing in the room.

Sarah glances at me sideways in a way I can't tell if she's about to laugh or reprimand me.

"What's happening?" I ask Sarah, whose husband remains intentionally "leaning back" and being easy-going in the session.

Sarah lets out a long sigh. "I miss the John I once knew in school." Her voice was quiet.

Once again, I hold back a temptation; this time to ask Sarah about what she means by that younger version of John.

Another thought has taken hold: "I wonder if you miss the Sarah you were back then."

"Not really," she answers.

There is a flatness in her response. John's frame tenses slightly, as if preparing to say something; to defend that younger Sarah she claims not to miss, perhaps? His mouth opens, as if ready to challenge or protect, but John focuses on the object in his hands, sinking back into the chair.

He is like the "good student!" I think silently.

"And what is it like to see John here with you now, offering to join you in therapy?" I ask Sarah.

John lifts his eyes towards Sarah.

"I want to enjoy this moment," her voice catches. "But something is stopping me from taking it in." Her fingers work at an invisible thread on her dress, a gesture that seems to unravel something deeper beyond fabric.

She then starts and stops several times, each false beginning like a door opening and quickly closing. "I never told anyone in therapy before…" she says. Pause. "I was eight." Pause. "My brother got to stay, but I—but I as a girl am dispensable."

Sarah's shoulders sag as her story breaks free. A tale of a little girl given away to another family, watching her brother remain with their mother and father. Her new home became a testing ground for survival—older step-siblings who viewed her as an intruder, endless household tasks that somehow always fell to her. "I was Cinderella. I learned to be useful," she smiles wryly. "Very, very useful." The pattern persisted even after growing up, completing her education, and establishing her career. As an adult, she cared for her adoptive mother through long illnesses, put her step-sisters' children through school, and became the family's emotional anchor.

"Feeling cared for, on the other hand," her voice now barely above a whisper, "is foreign to me."

"I feel overwhelmingly sad," I say. The vivid image in my mind of a child standing alone with her haphazardly packed shopping bag filled with clothes, sent away by her parents.

Sarah and I remain in a silence laden with too many words.

Still cradling the pink stress ball, John, a man who would "never dream of therapy," is still listening. He is the prince in Sarah's story. Tears trace silent paths down his weathered cheeks, falling freely, as if granted permission for the first time. I let the moment stretch, allowing them to feel the space between them.

He lets the pink object rest on his lap. His eyes focus on something far beyond the ceiling. Was he reaching back through decades to the school days he holds dear? He recounts the memories as they surface, clear and vivid: the girl in math class with her crown of spiky, gelled hair, her sharp wit that kept others at arm's length. In a school where most kids spoke Mandarin—a language that is not their mother tongue to both of them—they found common ground in the forbidden rhythms of Bronski Beat.

They shared secret moments listening to crackly BBC radio broadcasts, their ears pressed close to catch every note that Singapore's conservative stations wouldn't play in those days. Gender-bending artists like Bronski Beat were too controversial for local broadcast, but that only made the music more precious to the young rebels. They'd pool their pocket money to buy pirated cassette tapes at $2.50 each, treasuring these contraband sounds that spoke to their souls in ways the world around them wouldn't have understood.

In the room now, the nostalgic echoes of phantom synthesisers from the 80s float gently through the air, weaving their way around us like a tender embrace. It feels like we're lost in the hauntingly beautiful riff of "Smalltown Boy," each note stirring memories long tucked away. The space between us is now charged with electrifying energy, deeply saturated with unspoken words and emotions, making every heartbeat resonate in the rhythm of the melody.

As our time draws to a close, I notice Sarah's chair has somehow turned back toward John. They rise together, pensive. Sarah glances at the pink stress ball still in John's hands, as if to remind him. He looks down at it, then up at me.

"It's yours, now," I say.

Understanding Phenomenology Through Sarah and John's Session

The phenomenological approach came alive in Sarah and John's session through specific moments that showed how Gestalt therapy works with immediate experience rather than interpretation. When Sarah subtly adjusted her swivel chair—turning it slightly away while remaining engaged—a traditional therapist might have immediately labelled this as "avoidant attachment." Instead, the phenomenological stance encouraged curiosity: What was Sarah creating with this angle? How did this positioning reflect her way of being in relationship?

This exemplifies bracketing in practice. The therapist noticed her own assumptions wanting to arise—perhaps thoughts about defensive behaviour or relationship patterns—but held these in parentheses, setting them aside to stay with what was actually happening. This suspension of judgement allowed something more nuanced to emerge: Sarah's complex dance of yearning for connection while protecting herself from disappointment.

The pre-reflexive dimension revealed itself when the therapist felt compelled to reach for the pink stress ball. This was neither a planned intervention nor a meaningless impulse but an embodied response to the atmosphere of the therapeutic situation—a spontaneous impulse that arose before thought. John then shared a story his words couldn't yet articulate. As John was encouraged to go with his need to be "easy-going" his presence shifted and Sarah noticed: "I miss the John I once knew."

This is how the phenomenological attitude transforms couples therapy: by trusting that everything needed for healing is already present in the immediate moment, waiting to be witnessed rather than analysed, felt rather than fixed.

Here's a table that captures the key phenomenological concepts through Sarah and John's story:

Table 1.1 Phenomenological Principles in Practice

Phenomenological Principle	*How It Appeared in Session*	*What It Revealed*	*Traditional Approach Would Have...*
Bracketing	Therapist noticed assumptions about Sarah's chair positioning but held them in parentheses	Sarah's complex dance of yearning while self-protecting	Labelled it as "avoidant attachment" and prescribed corrective interventions
Pre-reflexive Awareness	Therapist's spontaneous impulse to reach for stress ball; John's fingers exploring texture	Body wisdom guiding the session before thought intervened	Planned a structured intervention or communication exercise, and therapist would have held herself from picking up the object
Atmosphere Sensing	Therapist felt "weightiness" in room; noticed rhythm disruption during Sarah's rapid speech	Decades of careful distance creating atmospheric density	Focused on individual anxiety or communication deficits
Present-moment Attunement	Invitation for John to "be easy-going" right now, following through from his mention of how he would like to be	Shift in John's mannerism inspired Sarah: "I miss the John I once knew"	Ignored/missed out the client's somewhat passing statement because of focus on getting to an outcome
Witnessing vs. Interpreting	John's tears received without analysis; shared music memory simply experienced	Profound meeting between two people rediscovering each other	Interpreted tears as breakthrough or breakdown (depending on the modality), "talking about" symbolism of teenage rebellion
Embodied Information	Therapist's somatic responses used as field information	Couple's unspoken patterns revealed through atmosphere	Dismissed therapist's sensations as countertransference to be managed
Shared Aesthetic Resonance	Phantom synthesizers from the 80s fill the room; therapist senses the music with them	Original connection resurfaces as living presence between them	Overlooked as trivial, analysed their teenage rebellion as defence, interpreted shared interests as compensation

In Sarah and John's story, the therapist's ability to resonate with Bronski Beat helped, with all three tuning into that shared aesthetic frequency. Had the music been unfamiliar to her, the therapist might have asked them to play it, allowing the actual sounds to fill the room. We use whatever supports us to tune in—music, movement, images, or chair work (which we'll explore in later chapters). The moment we shift into analysing, interpreting, or rushing toward solutions (which we usually would), we lose our presence to the phenomenon itself. We lose sight of the couple, replacing their living presence with effort and work.

Conclusion

There is a moment in every therapy when the air shifts. Words fall away. Defences soften. Something real emerges. For Sarah and John, it came as decades of careful distance collapsed into presence in the beat of music. Noticing these phenomena as it happens is the heart of practice.

Consider what didn't happen in their session. There was no need to analyse or intervene, no need to focus on teaching communication techniques. We didn't excavate the clients' childhood stories looking for explanations. Instead, we stayed present with Sarah's chair turning slightly away, John's fingers knotted in readiness, the weight in the room, the pink stress ball finding its way into his hands. We stayed with the living language of the therapeutic field.

The phenomenological stance emphasizes the transformative power of awareness itself. When Sarah could finally speak her truth—"Feeling cared for is foreign to me"—and when John could receive it with his whole being, something shifted that no technique could have orchestrated. This approach means surrendering the security of knowing, of having answers, of being the expert. We notice our own impulses—to comfort Sarah, to encourage John, to fill the silence—and use them as information about the field rather than directives for action.

The framework we've explored—attending to pre-contact patterns, atmospheric qualities, contact interruptions, embodied responses, and historical echoes—offers guidance without rigidity. Like a jazz musician who knows the changes but plays from inspiration, the phenomenological therapist uses these guideposts while remaining open to surprise.

Sarah and John left that session differently than they entered it. Not because they'd learned new skills or gained insights they could apply, but because they'd experienced themselves and each other anew—and paradoxically, connected with who they were innately.

While Sarah and John's story showed us how phenomenological witnessing opens up possibilities for contact, not all couples can access their shared history so readily. What happens when childhood adaptations to unbearable circumstances shape every attempt at intimacy? In the next chapter, as Liam reaches for another pint to escape overwhelm and Akina drifts into sleep just when he needs her most, we will see how trauma exists in the present, not just in the past. This phenomenological approach proves to be especially viable.

References

Husserl, E. (1913/2012). *Ideas: General introduction to pure phenomenology* (W. R. Boyce Gibson, Trans.). Dover Publications.

Perls, F., Hefferline, R. F., & Goodman, P. (1951). *Gestalt therapy: Excitement and growth in the human personality.* Julian Press.

Staemmler, F.-M. (2009). The willingness to be uncertain: Preliminary thoughts about interpretation and understanding in Gestalt therapy. In L. Jacobs & R. Hycner (Eds.), *Relational approaches in Gestalt therapy* (pp. 65–110). Gestalt Press.

Stern, D. N. (2004). *The present moment in psychotherapy and everyday life.* Norton.

2 Trauma in the Relational Field

"I get it. I get you. I get me."

—Liam

Trauma as Present-moment Phenomenon in Couples Therapy

When couples seek therapy, they often arrive with what appear to be communication problems, behavioral issues, or incompatibilities. Yet beneath these surface struggles, we frequently discover the living presence of trauma as immediate bodily experience shaping every interaction (Kepner, 2003; Levine, 2010; Taylor, 2014; van der Kolk, 2014). Trauma is not something that happened "back then" but persists in the here-and-now. Our understanding of trauma influences how we approach couples therapy. We're aware of its presence: a partner's body suddenly feeling heavy, their breath becoming shallow, their eyes losing focus just when a connection is most needed. These aren't "symptoms" to be dealt with, but what Perls, Hefferline, and Goodman (1951) call creative adjustments—unique ways each human being learns to cope with overwhelming circumstances experienced in early childhood (Resnick, 2020). A child whose academic survival depended on staying awake past exhaustion might develop a body that craves sleep as both an escape and a rebellion. A child whose parent disappeared might become hyper-vigilant, scanning every interaction for signs of impending abandonment. Traumatic childhood experiences such as these burn into children's nervous systems, becoming an invisible blueprint for their adult relationships.

The Therapeutic Situation as Resource

While some trauma therapies begin with extensive resourcing—such as teaching clients to imagine safe places, install bilateral stimulation, or develop coping strategies—Gestalt therapy understands that the therapeutic relationship itself is healing (Francesetti et al., 2013; Jacob & Hycner, 2009; Yontef, 1993). Bocian (2013) explores the idea of "the third," suggesting that what emerges between therapist and clients is not merely individuals in a room but a

DOI: 10.4324/9781003631545-4

co-created field with its own emergent properties. This living "third" presence, born from genuine contact and mutual engagement, provides the safety necessary for trauma work.

This differentiates Gestalt therapy fundamentally from approaches that construct safety through technique. EMDR's preparation phase, for instance, involves systematic installation of resources before processing traumatic material. While valuable in its context, this approach assumes safety must be imported from outside the immediate relationship, and the client is alone in this safe place. Gestalt therapy trusts that safety emerges from the quality of contact itself—the therapist's regulated presence, attuned responsiveness, and phenomenological stance.

Porges's (2011) polyvagal theory illuminates how relational safety can become challenging to traumatised individuals. When trauma has been shaped by relationship breakdown in early childhood, ordinary interactions within the relationship can register as dangerous. A partner's drowsiness might signal impending abandonment. A request for space might echo unbearable childhood loneliness. The therapeutic field, through the therapist's regulated nervous system and consistent presence, offers a different possibility: connection that doesn't threaten, presence that doesn't overwhelm.

Creative Adjustments in the Couple's Dance

Individual trauma patterns interlock to create relational choreography (Herman, 1992/2015; Johnson, 2002). One partner's need for distance triggers another's abandonment terror. One's hypervigilance exhausts another into withdrawal. These are each partner's survival strategies, influencing the other's in an endless loop.

The phenomenological approach encourages us to stay with these patterns, observing and feeling into the situation with curiosity. The therapist's attention to the patterns influences partners to unpack and view their responses to each other from another perspective—that conflict in the present is also an echo of the past. "This terror isn't about you leaving—it's my six-year-old self still waiting for my father." "This exhaustion isn't rejection—it's my body remembering when staying awake meant survival." These insights come from remaining phenomenologically present with embodied experience, allowing the wisdom of awareness itself to reveal what has remained hidden. In the story that follows, we meet Liam and Akina, who arrived in therapy seeking help with what seemed like a straightforward conflict—his drinking, her withdrawal. Yet as we'll witness, their present-day struggles revealed themselves as echoes of childhood adaptations, creative adjustments that once ensured survival but now created barriers to the very connection they seek. Through phenomenological attention to immediate experience, what began as a problem to solve transformed into an opportunity for deeper understanding and compassion.

Liam and Akina

They prop themselves on the edge of the leather couch, shoulders brushing against each other, Liam's hand protectively covering Akina's in his lap. Their physical contrasts are striking: Akina, with her delicate frame and pale complexion, has long black hair cascading around her shoulders, while Liam, muscular and tanned, radiates a masculine energy that speaks of his successful transition.

"I've been drinking a lot more these past few weeks." Liam's voice is deep. His words linger between us; the admission eases and disturbs him. "That's why I wanted Akina to join us today. She needs to understand from you how she can help me out."

This is my first meeting with Akina, though I've heard much about her through Liam's sessions. Her gaze has a soft sleepiness as she slightly bows in acknowledgement. "Yes, I want to help," she says carefully, her accent shaping her words. She leans almost imperceptibly toward Liam when she speaks as if drawn to him by an invisible thread.

Liam has been out drinking more frequently—a theme in his previous therapy sessions. Life for him has been a whirlwind of changes: a new job demanding more from him, an apartment renovation proving more stressful than anticipated, and, of course, the physical and emotional adjustments following his gender confirmation surgeries.

They both bear their burdens. Akina is grappling with anxiety, adjusting to and seeking employment in the country. Now that they are newly married, their love is a bright spot amidst all this upheaval, yet it adds another layer of complexity to their busy lives.

I lean forward slightly in my chair, taking in the picture before me—two people holding on to each other. The air conditioner hums softly in the background.

"Tell me more about what's happening," My speech deliberate.

"After dinner, I feel the need to…vanish to the coffee shop downstairs. I would have a couple of pints of beer." His thumb traces small circles on Akina's hand as he speaks, as if to reassure her or perhaps himself.

"And I cannot come along," Akina interjects. Her eyes meet mine briefly before they drop to their intertwined hands. "I think he spends too much… time drinking."

Liam's shoulders tighten as he keeps his voice steady. "I feel overwhelmed at the office; my boss keeps pushing us to complete these pointless tasks, just churning out work that appears good on paper but holds no real value." His free hand gestures in frustration. "And when Akina and I argue…" He looks at her. "It's incredibly draining for me. I need to take a break and be on my own. Those pints help me find quiet. Away."

Akina's body is now heavier against Liam's side, and her eyelids begin to droop. Though her hand remains in his, her presence seems to be receding, like a tide slowly pulling away from shore. Is she perhaps exhausted from following our conversation in English?

Liam's eyes flick anxiously to Akina, his grip on her hand tightening slightly. He mutters a "hmm."

"Yes, yes," Akina murmurs back, nodding slowly, though it's unclear whether she's responding to Liam or something in her thoughts.

I am uncertain about what they are trying to convey, and I check if there is something I am missing.

"Yes, yes," Akina repeats.

An inertia settles over the room. I feel the tension between clinging and retreating, staying and slipping away. *Should we call Akina back into presence or honour her retreat?* I stay with the discomfort.

The atmosphere surrounding us feels fragile. Unarticulated thoughts stretch the space. I want to understand her "yes," but the energy for such a conversation is low.

Akina's body slackens, melting into Liam's side. Instinctively, he straightens, his grip tightening as hers loosens—a sleepy dance—her slow retreat, his unconscious bracing against it.

Liam and I talk at a carefully controlled pace. He reveals that this slower tempo of conversation contrasts with his instinct to dive headfirst into tasks and manage everything at once.

Akina's gaze drifts off as he speaks further. Her posture gradually slumps into a hunch. "I'm sorry," she says abruptly, glancing at Liam and smiling.

"I just get so triggered," he says, thoughtlessly gripping a clump of his hair with his free hand.

"She'll say she's taking a fifteen-minute nap, but three hours later, she's still in bed." His voice trails off. He then explains that it's worse for him when she tries to fight her sleepiness, forcing herself to stay awake "out of obligation." "She's physically there but completely absent."

"Like now?" I ask.

Liam's eyes flick to Akina, then to me. He looks away.

"What happens to you when she does this now?"

He exhales, slow and uneven. His usual quick responses stall. "Strange…" He swallows. "The only word I can think of is…unsafe."

The word lands in the space between us, heavier than expected. This is a man who has fought for his identity, endured medical interventions, and navigated hostile workplaces, yet his partner's drifting away unsettles him the most. His voice lowers.

"Unloved." A pause. "Lonely."

Akina's eyes well up. "But I'm here," she says and rubs Liam's arm.

"Yes," says Liam, "but I feel like I'm too much."

"Too much?" I ask.

"A burden," says Liam.

"Yes, just a little," Akina attempts a smile.

"A little?" I gesture with my hand, thumb nearly touching the tip of my index finger.

"No. Actually. Very tired. I don't know." Akina says.

Liam shares what he knows of Akina's childhood—the gruelling reality of the Korean cram school, where academic excellence came at the cost of basic needs like sleep and play. "The teachers would make them stay awake past midnight to study if they failed practice exams, and they would sleep on the classroom floor because of exhaustion," he explains, his protective instinct evident in his tone. "Her parents were always working, so she and her brother lived with an aunt close to the cram school."

Akina explains that staying awake means "surviving" in the place. "Sleep was..." she sighs. "Risky."

A pause. A breath. Then, softer: "Also, a way to disappear."

"You don't seem to be disappearing right now," I say.

"Oh, no," she smiles.

I turn to Liam, "This feeling you mentioned of being unsafe...I am wondering if it reminds you of another time."

He blinks. Breathes in. His voice is hoarse. "My father." The words hover, fragile.

"Please elaborate," I say to him.

"They divorced," he begins. "He tried to stay close, to still see us. Until I was six, then he simply disappeared."

"Oh." Akina and I gasp, almost in unison.

"My mother and her extended family never revealed anything to us. She told people that he had gone to work abroad."

Liam's story unfolds gradually: his father tried to keep in touch until it became emotionally impossible for him to do so. He found a home in an Indian commune, where he accidentally overdosed. This was revealed to Liam when an older relative showed him a handwritten note.

Liam's story deeply moved me, as I had pieced together fragments during our sessions. It wasn't until today, however, that I genuinely grasped how he continues to cope with the impact of his father's disappearance and death, alongside the family's need to conceal these events.

I grasp now how his father's gradual fading echoes in his body whenever Akina slowly disappears into sleep.

I am torn between waking Akina to bring her back "online" and protecting her refuge from a lifetime of relentless demands. Their physical connection—his tightening grip and her leaning body—offers a temporary bridge across this gap while preventing them from moving freely.

As Akina acknowledges Liam's childhood wounds of abandonment, and as Liam grasps the depth of Akina's exhaustion from years of enforced wakefulness, their symptoms become meaningful to each other rather than threatening.

In our following sessions, Liam's view of his father shifted. "He tried hard to be what everyone expected him to be." He pauses. "Like me."

His hand drifts to his chest, "A wife, children, a whole life built on denial. And still, he tried to stay with us...until he couldn't."

He swallows at the realisation that doesn't erase his grief, instead sharpening it. If only he had been older. If only he could have spoken the words back then.

"Pa," he whispers, more to himself than to us. "I get it. I get you. I get me." Holding absence and presence, loss and love, I exhale, moved.

Witnessing Individual Trauma in the Relationship

The phenomenological approach revealed itself from the very first moments of contact. Before words could articulate their struggles, the nature of their relationship declared itself through their bodies: Liam's protective hand covering Akina's, their shoulders touching yet somehow conveying distance, the contrast between his muscular vigilance and her delicate drowsiness. The atmosphere exhibited particular qualities: a delicate tension between clinging and retreating, an exhaustion seeming to fill the air, the feeling of two people desperately holding on while also pulling away. The therapist's uncertainty about what they were attempting to express became a valuable insight—trauma often communicates through confusion, mixed signals, and bodies conveying what words cannot.

Creative Adjustments Meeting Creative Adjustments

Liam's visit to the coffee shop for "a couple of pints" was more than just avoiding something. His drinking served as a form of withdrawal—an inventive way to handle intense emotions. Likewise, Akina's drowsiness wasn't simply tiredness; it was her body's conditioned reaction to stress, reminiscent of years spent awake in cram schools where sleep was both banned and her only relief.

These patterns represent creative adjustments—brilliant adaptations to unbearable childhood circumstances that become our personality patterns. Once-necessary survival strategies that protected us as children often become obsolete, even harmful, in adult relationships. We unconsciously reenact these coping mechanisms with our partners, creating cycles of disconnection where connection is desperately sought.

These patterns of creative adjustment reveal themselves clearly when we trace their journey from childhood survival to adult relationship dynamics:

Table 2.1 Creative Adjustments: From Survival to Relationship Patterns

Childhood Experience	*Creative Adjustment*	*Adult Relational Pattern*	*Impact on Partner*
Forced wakefulness in cram school	Sleep as escape/rebellion	Drowsiness when overwhelmed	Partner feels abandoned/unsafe
Father's gradual disappearance	Hypervigilance for abandonment	Tightening grip, anxiety when partner withdraws	Partner feels suffocated/guilty
Academic pressure without rest	Body shuts down under stress	"Checking out" during conflict	Partner experiences as rejection
Family conceal the nature of father's absence	Scanning for truth/safety	Excessive need for reassurance	Partner feels inadequate/untrusted

The therapist maintained a phenomenological stance, witnessing these patterns without interpretation. There was no need to wonder if Liam's drinking was pathological or Akina's sleepiness dissociative. By attending to the immediate experience—one partner gradually receding from consciousness while the other's anxiety visibly increased—space was created for the patterns to reveal their deeper meaning.

When Past and Present Collide

The pivotal moment came with a single word. When asked what happens when Akina drifts away, Liam struggled before landing on "unsafe." This word became a portal to his childhood experience. The therapist's phenomenological attention to this word, rather than rushing past it, allowed its full significance to emerge.

"Unsafe" revealed memories of a child, six years old, whose father gradually vanished, whose family covered up his absence. The word became a bridge between past and present, showing how Akina's withdrawal activated ancient terror in Liam's nervous system. As psychoanalysis (Freud, 1912) has long recognised, we transfer past relationships onto present ones—seeing our critical mother in our partner's feedback, hearing our absent father in their silence.

As their stories unfolded, the somatic aspect of trauma became obvious. Akina's body had learned that staying awake meant "surviving," but sleep was also "a way to disappear." Her nervous system carried these conflicting survival strategies into adulthood. Liam's body remained hypervigilant for signs of abandonment—his tightening grip as Akina dozed, his unconscious bracing against her retreat, his need to "vanish" when overwhelmed.

Throughout the session, the contrast between what their bodies revealed and what their words expressed illuminated the hidden language of trauma:

Table 2.2 Trauma's Language: Body vs. Words

What the Body Shows	*What Words Say*	*The Hidden Message*	*Relational Impact*
Akina melts into Liam's side	"Yes, I want to help"	"I'm disappearing to survive"	Liam feels abandoned despite physical closeness
Liam grips hair, tightens hold	"I need space to drink"	"Don't leave me like my father did"	Akina feels responsible for his distress
Slow, heavy movements	"Just a little tired"	"My body remembers enforced exhaustion"	Misread as lack of care
Anxious eye movements	"She needs to understand"	"I'm scanning for signs you'll leave"	Creates the very distance feared

Witnessing

During couples therapy, we create space for individual exploration while maintaining awareness of the relational field. The therapist might focus attention on one partner while the other remains present as a witness. This isn't passive observation—the therapist continuously checks how the witnessing partner is impacted, creating a triangulated dialogue where both individual experience and relational impact are honoured.

Some of Liam's deeper exploration of his father's absence occurred in individual sessions—a decision made collectively when the material felt extensive. When they regrouped, Akina could witness and respond to Liam's process with the support of the therapeutic container. This alternating focus allows each partner to process individual trauma while recognising that the intensity of their reactions has historical roots.

From Isolation to Recognition

The transformation began when each could witness the other's pattern with compassion rather than threat. When partners recognise "This terror isn't about you—it's my body remembering my father leaving" or "This exhaustion isn't rejection—it's my body remembering when staying awake meant survival," something profound shifts. They begin to see each other clearly, perhaps for the first time, freed from the ghosts of past relationships.

In subsequent sessions, Liam's understanding deepened. "He tried hard to be what everyone expected him to be. Like me." This wasn't intellectual insight but embodied recognition—feeling in his own chest the weight his father must have carried, integrating the split between past and present.

Therapy didn't eradicate trauma's effects but lit a candle in the darkness that concealed it. Akina might still grow drowsy when overwhelmed; Liam might still feel waves of ancient fear. But now these responses exist in their awareness. They do not define the relationship; instead, they echo childhood survival strategies now obsolete in adulthood.

Their journey from mutual triggering to mutual understanding unfolded through distinct stages of recognition:

Table 2.3 From Individual Trauma to Shared Understanding

Stage of Recognition	*Liam's Process*	*Akina's Process*	*Relational Shift*
Surface Complaint	"She sleeps too much"	"He drinks too much"	Mutual blame
First Awareness	"I feel unsafe"	"I feel exhausted"	Beginning empathy
Deeper Recognition	"Like when father left"	"Like cram school"	Seeing patterns
Embodied Understanding	"Pa tried to stay connected"	"Sleep was my only escape"	Compassion emerges
Integration	"I get you. I get me"	"I'm not abandoning you"	New possibility

Out of the isolating darkness, healing happens from truly being seen, especially by someone loved.

Conclusion

"Pa, I get it. I get you. I get me." In these whispered words lies the transformative power of phenomenological witnessing. Liam didn't just understand his father's struggles intellectually—he felt the resonance in his bones, recognising their shared humanity. His father, trapped in a life that didn't fit, had tried to maintain connection until the pain became unbearable. Now Liam could see his own hypervigilance not as pathology but as a child's desperate attempt to prevent the unpreventable.

What brought them to therapy—his drinking, her sleeping—seemed like surface problems with obvious solutions. Yet by staying with immediate phenomena, something deeper emerged. Akina's enforced wakefulness in cram schools created a body that sought sleep as both escape and rebellion. Liam's father's disappearance left him scanning for abandonment in every withdrawal. These weren't problems to fix but creative adjustments revealing themselves through present-moment experience. When we stay present with what is, the past announces itself through the body, through patterns, through the very atmosphere between people. The phenomenological stance creates spaciousness for discovery rather than diagnosis, trusting that awareness itself catalyses change.

As we turn to Chapter 3, we'll explore how this patience becomes essential when couples desperately seek change. What happens when staying with "what is" feels impossible? Beisser's (1970) Paradoxical Theory of Change offers a radical proposition: transformation comes not from trying to be different, but from fully accepting who we already are.

References

Beisser, A. (1970). The paradoxical theory of change. In J. Fagan & I. L. Shepherd (Eds.), *Gestalt therapy now* (pp. 77–80). Science and Behavior Books.

Bocian, B. (2013). From free association to concentration: About alienation, Ferenczi's "forced fantasies," and "he third" in Gestalt therapy. *Gestalt Theory*, 35(1), 49–64. https://doi.org/10.2478/gth-2013-0005

Francesetti, G., Gecele, M., & Roubal, J. (Eds.). (2013). *Gestalt therapy in clinical practice: From psychopathology to the aesthetics of contact.* FrancoAngeli.

Freud, S. (1912). The dynamics of transference. In *The standard edition of the complete psychological works of Sigmund Freud*, 12(97), 108. Hogarth Press.

Herman, J. L. (1992/2015). *Trauma and recovery: The aftermath of violence—from domestic abuse to political terror.* Basic Books.

Jacobs, L. & Hycner, R. (Eds.). (2009). *Relational approaches in Gestalt therapy.* Gestalt Press.

Johnson, S. M. (2002). *Emotionally focused couple therapy with trauma survivors: Strengthening attachment bonds.* Guilford Press.

Kepner, J. I. (2003). *Body process: A Gestalt approach to working with the body in psychotherapy.* Gestalt Institute of Cleveland Press.

Levine, P. A. (2010). *In an unspoken voice: How the body releases trauma and restores goodness*. North Atlantic Books.
Perls, F. S., Hefferline, R. F., & Goodman, P. (1951). *Gestalt therapy: Excitement and growth in the human personality*. Julian Press.
Porges, S. W. (2011). *The polyvagal theory: Neurophysiological foundations of emotions, attachment, communication, and self-regulation*. W. W. Norton & Company.
Resnick, R. W. (2020). *A couple of individuals: Introduction to Gestalt therapy [Video]*. YouTube. https://www.youtube.com/watch?v=gXG8DOtmmlk&t
Taylor, D. (2014). *Embodied relating: The ground of psychotherapy*. PCCS Books.
van der Kolk, B. A. (2014). *The body keeps the score: Brain, mind, and body in the healing of trauma*. Viking.
Yontef, G. (1993). *Awareness, dialogue and process: Essays on Gestalt therapy*. The Gestalt Journal Press.

Part II

The Paradox of Change

3 The Paradoxical Theory of Change in Couples Work

"I am looking for an outcome here."

—Markus

Core Theory: Beisser's Paradoxical Theory of Change in Couples Therapy

When couples enter therapy, they arrive with urgent demands for solutions. "Fix our communication" or "Stop us from fighting" are common requests. "Tell us what to do" is a frequent ask. Therapists feel the pressing need to offer immediate solutions, which reflects a fundamental misunderstanding about how genuine relationship transformations happen with couples therapy. The problem is that the harder partners try to force themselves or each other to be different, the more entrenched their struggles become.

Arnold Beisser's (1970) paradoxical theory of change offers a radical alternative to this effortful striving. In his seminal essay, Beisser articulated what would become a cornerstone of Gestalt therapy: "Change does not take place by 'trying,' coercion, or persuasion, or by insight, interpretation, or any other such means. Rather, change can occur when the patient abandons, at least for the moment, what he would like to become and attempts to be what he is" (p. 77).

This principle emerged from Beisser's unique vantage point as both a therapist trained by Fritz Perls and a person living with polio who intimately understood the futility of fighting against "what is." As Perls (1969/1992) put it,

> [W]e realize that we cannot deliberately bring about changes in ourselves or in others. [...] Many people dedicate their lives to actualize a concept of what they should be like, rather than to actualize themselves. [...] Where some people have a self, most people have a void, because they are so busy projecting themselves as this or that. This is again the curse of the ideal. The curse that you should not be what you are.
>
> (p. 39)

DOI: 10.4324/9781003631545-6

This insight revolutionised our understanding of therapeutic change: transformation paradoxically occurs not through efforts to become different, but through the full acceptance and awareness of our present reality.

The theory appears paradoxical because it contradicts our instinctive problem-solving approaches. When something is wrong, we naturally want to fix it. When we're in pain, we seek immediate relief. Yet in relationships, this fixing mentality often perpetuates the very patterns couples seek to escape. Each partner tries to change the other, creating cycles of blame, resistance, and disappointment. The relationship becomes a battlefield of competing change agendas.

The onus is on the therapist to resist the pressure to "help" create change and inadvertently perpetuate the couple's problems. Yontef (1992) elaborated, "When the therapist rejects the change agent role, change that is orderly and also meaningful is possible" (p. 141). The therapist's rejection of the change agent role does not mean therapeutic passivity. Rather, it signifies an active stance of supporting couples to fully experience and understand their current reality—the actual texture of their conflicts, the genuine nature of their differences, and the authentic quality of their connection or disconnection.

In the pages that follow, we'll witness this paradoxical principle unfold through the lives of two couples facing distinct yet interconnected challenges. Mei and Markus arrive demanding solutions for their "communication problem," yet beneath this request lies a deeper struggle with cultural differences and unacknowledged grief. Their story reveals how the pressure to force change—his demand for her to embrace his children, her silent withdrawal from expectations that echo a lifetime of caretaking—only entrenches their disconnection. Meanwhile, Sherlyn and Derrick present with a different kind of urgency: three years of marriage without physical intimacy. Their journey illuminates how invisible audiences—the internalised voices of family, church, and community—can crowd the most intimate spaces, making genuine contact impossible until these phantom observers are acknowledged rather than ignored.

Both couples demonstrate the same paradoxical truth: the harder we try to eliminate what troubles us, the more firmly it takes root. Yet when therapist and clients together can resist the siren call of quick fixes and instead stay present with the full reality of their struggles, something unexpected emerges. Not the change they thought they wanted, but the transformation they actually need.

Case Study A: Mei and Markus—Cultural Boundaries

"We aren't communicating," Markus announces, claiming an armchair. The accent in his words makes his agitation seem more intense. As he arranges himself on his seat, his blue eyes sweep the room, assessing. He is a therapy veteran.

"It's become quite difficult for us," Mei says, her tone slow, measured. She is, after all, a Human Resources professional apt at managing corporate crises at work. She settles into her chair, smoothing her pencil skirt with freshly manicured hands. A few years past fifty, she carries herself with a grace that renders age irrelevant.

"Difficult?" I ask.

"It's been difficult since the twins visited last month," Markus says. A muscle twitches in his jaw. "They have gone back to Germany now with their mother."

"That's Ulrike," says Mei.

"Yes, my ex-wife," Markus confirms, his jaw tightening slightly. "She and the children went back after...well...after my transfer to Singapore didn't work out how we'd planned."

Mei's interlaced fingers press lightly on her lap. "Markus and I met shortly after that," she says, emphasizing the word "after." "Both of us are starting over."

She continues with a small, wry smile, "On a dating app, of all places."

"The modern way," Markus strains a laugh.

"Sixteen years with my previous partner," Mei says, her tone matter of fact. "We never married. It was...different."

"Different, how?" I ask.

"He was very Singaporean Chinese. Although I'm also Chinese, our expectations of one another were..." She pauses, searching for the right words, "strangely less aligned, perhaps. But with Markus..." She glances at him, and a softness crosses her face.

"I am looking for an outcome here," Markus cuts in, his tone pointed. I observe Mei and I flinch. He continues, "I know you're good at what you do; you must be, given your reputation. Just tell us what we should do."

His demanding tone crashes on me. *Something to ponder later in supervision*, I think to myself. I reach for my cup of mint tea and take a sip of it. I lean back, creating some space for myself.

"What do you think you should do right now?" I ask.

His shoulders drop slightly. "I don't know. I don't know. I guess I'll just have to sit here and see what happens."

"And that wouldn't be so bad an idea," I say.

"That's exactly it," Markus retorts, "She shuts herself off."

"Can you define what 'it' is?" I ask deliberately.

Markus's face contorts. "I can't understand," he says, seeming exasperated. "I hope you're not merely buying time..."

"Responding to my question will help us understand your situation better. And it's entirely your choice, Markus," I say.

"It is because she doesn't make the effort to get to know my kids. At least play with them," he sighs.

"And that is important to you, for Mei to...interact with your kids." I pause, letting his words settle. I suggest that he say this directly to Mei.

Markus turns towards Mei and says, "It is important to me that you like my kids."

Mei responds with a smile, yet her eyes remain still. Her reply unfolds, each detail adding depth to the image. "I am the eldest of five," she states, her usual corporate polish slipping away. Turning to me, she says, "You know, in my family, that signifies something." The weight of her parents' disappointment now tones her voice. "Everything was always so serious, so heavy with consequence." She straightens her already impeccable posture. "When I finally bought my first apartment…"—which she had to wait until she reached thirty-five to afford—"It was a relief. Those four walls were mine alone. No one to care for but myself." She glances at Markus softly, almost apologetically. "At forty-eight, meeting you…I believed I was finally ready to share space."

The rhythm of her childhood home echoes: "We were quiet children. We did our homework, ate our meals, and dressed ourselves. Being good meant being obedient and quiet. It meant staying out of our parents' way." She smooths an invisible crease from her skirt. "Yes, I thought I was there, available to your children. But they are kids and aren't so responsive to me."

"But they will be; they are always ready to meet people," Markus interjects.

"What is Mei's relationship with their mother?" I ask.

Markus's shoulders slump.

"I try not to get in the way," Mei answers, each word sounding well-chosen.

I feel many responses bubbling up inside me—solutions, suggestions, interpretations—but I hold them back, knowing that would be too soon. "I would like to offer you all sorts of recommendations right now," I tell Markus honestly, "and I know that the best way to support you now is to help you connect with each other. I'm wondering if both of you are up for it."

"In my family," Markus begins, "people talk." His hands sculpt the air as he speaks, as if trying to shape the invisible distance between his upbringing and Mei's traditional background. "We're encouraged to share our thoughts and be transparent. Our family constantly engages in activities together."

"My father," he says, and I notice how his posture straightens instinctively, "he's a pastor in the village where we live. Everything we did was visible. Public."

"The pastor's family, I imagine, is a kind of model?" I check.

The parsonage stood next to the church, their private life always visible through its French windows. On Sundays, the congregation would filter through the home after the service, his mother's coffee and cake transforming their sitting room into an extension of the church community. Markus learned early on that family meant being available, present, and open. "My sisters and I, way into our late teens, were expected to join these gatherings to demonstrate the warmth and unity that a pastor's family should embody," Markus explains, and a complex emotion crosses his face.

"She managed everything in detail," he continues, "how we appeared to the congregation. My mother knows everyone." A slight note of what sounds like bitterness enters his voice. "She entertains, and there were always people at our house, always together, always sharing."

"Being the youngest," he adds, glancing at Mei, "with two older sisters…it was…" He searches for words, his English momentarily inadequate for the complexity of his experience. "I was always catching up. Running behind."

Mei reacts, subtly tilting her head.

"The anxiety started early," Markus continues, his right hand unconsciously moving in an erasing motion. "At school, I couldn't stop erasing my work—again and again—until the paper…" He mimics tearing. "The teachers noticed. Then came the therapy. But even now…" His fingers drum against the armrest, that same restless energy seeking an outlet. "And now, with Mei, there's this block. No talking about feelings. It's like…"

"And now your family is somewhat separated," I say, struck by the contrast between his childhood scene and his children's.

"What do you mean?" Markus asks sharply.

"Well, your children are a 12-hour flight away," I repeat.

"I go up once every two months to see them…" his words tumbling out.

"Yes," I say. I am touched by a tinge of sadness, recalling a time in my childhood when my dad went away on business trips, "And they remain a 12-hour flight away."

This silence carries weight, not the confrontational silence of resistance, but something more gentle. Markus's shoulders fall slightly, as if he's been holding back a truth he's now allowing himself to feel. Mei shatters it by clearing her throat, her gaze sharp with intensity. A part of her awakens.

"And I am not their mother," she asserts, each word precise.

"Yes," I say.

Markus's body stiffens. He opens his mouth to speak, but Mei's calm, confident voice seems to anchor him. For the first time since they entered my office, genuine communication feels possible between them.

"I have spent my whole life being responsible for children who aren't my own," Mei states clearly. "And now," she fixes her gaze on Markus, holding the calm that has protected her for years, but there's a new sense of strength in her demeanour—a firmness that wasn't present before.

The initial rush of energy that pushed Markus into my office, seeking solutions for their "communication problem," has subsided. Mei is now communicating, but not in the way he anticipated. This isn't the outcome they were hoping for. I reflect this to them as we conclude.

Sharing their truths reveals their core differences—namely, her need for boundaries around family involvement and his strong reluctance to face the difficult emotions linked to his separation from his children. They resemble two dancers finding their rhythm, not through perfectly matching steps but by honouring each other's unique movements.

Change for Happened Mei and Markus When…

The paradoxical theory of change is revealed through the interaction between Mei and Markus. They arrived seeking solutions to their "communication problem," yet the fundamental transformation began when they stopped trying to fix anything. When Markus finally heard "I am not their mother," something shifted—not because Mei offered a solution, but because she fully inhabited her truth

This reflects Beisser's insight: change occurs when we embrace who we truly are, rather than trying to become something we're not. Mei didn't have to force herself into a maternal role she had spent years avoiding, nor did she need to escape it through silence. Markus didn't require techniques to encourage her to connect with his children. Instead, they needed to fully experience their differences—her aversion to caregiving and his sorrow over separation—without rushing to fix these issues.

Observe how the therapist avoided giving Markus quick answers. Instead of offering solutions, she allowed what was already there to come to the surface. This approach isn't passive; it actively trusts that awareness alone can trigger change. When couples fully experience their patterns instead of analysing them, and feel their struggles instead of merely strategising, a natural process begins to unfold.

While Mei and Markus grapple with cultural expectations and geographical distance, our next couple faces a different barrier to connection. For three years, Sherlyn and Derrick have lived as married roommates, their intimacy interrupted by forces they cannot name or escape. Their story shows how the same paradoxical principle applies: the invisible audiences crowding their most private moments will continue their interference until fully acknowledged, not eliminated.

Case Study B: Sherlyn and Derrick—Intimacy Interrupted

"I freeze," Sherlyn whispers, recounting the moments they desire intimacy. She sits upright on the armchair's edge, her slender fingers resting stiffly on her lap.

"It is difficult for me when this happens." Derrick adjusts his wire-rimmed glasses, a gesture that seems habitual. "Then I can't continue… It reminds me of my parents." His father occasionally attempted to be affectionate with his mother by touching her hand or saying something endearing, only for her to pull away. His mother would express openly that she no longer found her husband attractive.

Their presence in the room evokes the solemn ambience of a stately parliament chamber. Putting aside the pressure building inside me to "do something," I take a moment to observe how strikingly similar they are—both are very slim and fair-complexioned, wearing identical wire-frame glasses on their noses. With their mirrored postures, they could easily be mistaken for siblings. Their body language hints at a shared history, maintaining a careful distance from each other while seemingly magnetically aligned.

Sherlyn carefully pauses to choose her words, "We've been married for three years" Her fingers twist the simple gold band on her left hand.

Derrick manages a quiet "Yes."

Then, a heavy silence fills the room. I wait. Finally, Sherlyn speaks again, her voice so low I needed to lean forward slightly to hear: "We have not even been intimate."

Their revelation doesn't catch me off guard. What surprises me more is how quickly they addressed the issue.

"How do you envision my support helping you both move forward?" I ask, anticipating no response. This question weighs on my thoughts.

The two partners glance at me, identical looks of slight surprise appearing on their faces. Their synchronization…

"I just said something surprising?" I check, curious about their reaction.

"I suppose," Derrick ventures, fingertips adjusting his glasses again, "it's your frankness. You didn't pretend there was some protocol or that you had an immediate solution."

I appreciate his reflection. "This is perhaps where intimacy begins," I add, "the courage to be real, and taking time before rushing into things."

Both partners exhale, relaxing their shoulders. The atmosphere starts to thaw.

"I'm curious about your experience right now, being here," I encourage them to scan the room. The air conditioning hums, a gentle counterpoint to the weighted silence that follows my question.

Sherlyn glances at Derrick before responding. "It feels…exposing, but also somewhat relieving." They have never spoken about their intimate issues with anyone before.

"Not even with your cell group leaders?" I ask, referencing their church involvement, though I have a sense of what their answer will be.

"Especially not them," Derrick responds with a quick shudder. "Everyone there has kids already. They keep asking when we're going to start our family."

"So much pressure," Sherlyn adds, curling her shoulders. "Every Sunday, someone will pat my belly and say, 'When, ah?'"

"And Lyn's mother has started insinuating that we check out fertility specialists." Derrick chimes in.

"Without checking if it is okay with you first?" I inquire, observing how his jaw tightens at the mention of his mother-in-law's interference.

"My mother-in-law means well," he states while the tension in his neck betrays his discomfort. "She's always been very…involved in Lyns…in all her daughters' lives, actually."

"She wants us to try IVF," Sherlyn's voice cracks. "But how can we when we haven't even…" Her voice trails off into space.

"What's it like having family so deeply involved?" I wiggle my shoulders as if needing to make space.

"It's normal for us," Sherlyn sighs. "All my sisters lived at home till after getting married, some even months after. My older sister only moved out of the family home when she had her second child. And it's because our parents frowned at us renting our own place while we wait for our purchased apartment to be built."

Home feels crowded. I notice my own chest tightening, as if the walls of my office have somehow drawn closer. The air itself seems dense with uninvited presences. I thought to myself. "How do you feel about all this?" I ask.

"Mom gets upset if we even dare to go shopping without her," Sherlyn explains, skillfully sidestepping the emotional gist of my question. "She needs to be involved in everything we do, even buying personal things."

She glances at her phone. Mom just sent a message on the family chat.

"What do you imagine Derrick's slouch is saying about his feelings?" I ask Sherlyn, noticing Derrick's posture.

She scans him, slouched on the couch, closely looking at him, perhaps for the first time since they arrived. She brings her slim hands to her mouth and giggles, her eyes suddenly alive with warmth. "Aiyoh, he looks so *sian*!" she exclaims, employing the Singlish term for utter indignant resignation.

Derrick's eyes light up. Sherlyn's candidness is a surprise. Their shared laughter feels transformative creating a spark, precious and fleeting.

"We've been condo-shopping," Sherlyn offers tentatively.

"But it's complicated," Derrick adds quickly, his smile fading. "With my father..."

"What I'm hearing," I say, leaning forward very slightly, "is that there's very little space just for the two of you. In your marriage, there seems to be many people involved."

Sherlyn's gaze meets Derrick's.

"We do have our travels," she says, "Those times when we're away, it feels different."

"Different, how?"

"Free," Derrick replies, "Like we can breathe. No one is checking what time we come home, and no one is asking about our plans."

"Yet even in that freedom," I venture, "intimacy remains challenging?"

I notice a slight flush beneath the foundation on Sherlyn's cheeks. "When we're close, I sense...something isn't right."

"Tell me if this fits: When we get close, I sense...?" I say.

"I feel...off. Weird. Cringe," she answers.

I ask her about the tension.

She tenses her torso, clenches her jaws, and fists. Her body now resembles a tautly wound cord.

Her eyes widen. "People are watching," she inhales deeply. "There are the people...my mother, the church ladies, everyone. I know they're not really here, but..."

"Yet..." I say.

"I feel watched. That's how it feels," sighs Sherlyn.

"The people watching, I wonder if we should invite them," I ask.

Derrick exhales loudly. Then, almost to himself, he murmurs, "Hah...yes."

"If they were to be here now," I say, sounding like a school teacher telling a story, "What would it be like for you, Sherlyn?"

"I don't know," Sherlyn mutters.

"Offer them seats." Derrick springs a grin.

The couple observes with a mixture of curiosity and apprehension as I leave my seat. I gather chairs from the stack in a corner and arrange them into a loose semicircle. The scraping of chairs pulled from the stack seems to echo their years of dragging invisible watchers through their marriage. We decide who will sit on which chair: Sherlyn's mother, the church ladies, and, at the other end, Derrick's mother and father. The invisible audience that has haunted their marriage now takes tangible form on the laid-out plastic chairs.

"This feels so creepy," Derrick says, smirking at the chairs, his arms wrapped around himself. "Yet it makes perfect sense. This is exactly how it feels every time. Like we're never truly alone."

Sherlyn gazes at the empty chairs, considering them in silence. Her composure fractures, exposing a raw and honest "Ugh! I just hate it!"

"What is 'it'?" I point to the group of empty chairs. "Better still, tell them directly what you hate."

"I hate that you are all sitting here," she says, her voice growing. The words are a surprise to her as she speaks them.

"What do you need?" I ask.

"I want you to leave." Her voice trembles and strengthens with each syllable. "All of you. Go. Just go. Just go!" Tears flow down her cheeks.

Derrick watches on with awe, his eyes glistening.

In silence, I take the moment in.

Derrick puts a hand on his wife's lap, stroking it gently.

"You can also make them leave," I say.

Derrick rises slowly, moving toward the chair that represents his father, intending to return it to the stack, but as he gets close, his body freezes mid-motion. "I can't do it," he says, the words catching in his throat. He leaves the chair where it stands and retreats to his seat, defeated.

"What stops you at this moment?" I ask.

Derrick's eyes are fixed on "his father's" chair. His chest feels tight. I notice he is not breathing, so I subtly remind him to.

"Perhaps you have something to tell him," I add.

"Ba," he starts, then pauses, removing his glasses to wipe his eyes. Through tears, he continues, "You lost everything when Ma left. I don't want you to lose me, too."

Touched by Derrick's words, I turn to Sherlyn, whose earlier outburst has settled into something quieter but no less intense. Her tears have slowed, but her breathing remains uneven. The forceful anger of her earlier "Leave!" seems to have drained away, leaving behind something more complex.

"Perhaps you have something to say to your mother before asking her to leave this room," I say.

"Mom," she says to "her mother's" empty chair, her voice carrying years of unspoken truth. "I need space. You say you care, but I think you are there for yourself." Her voice catches on to this revelation. "I want you to step away. I don't want to be afraid of you anymore."

Sherlyn stands up steadily. She lifts the chair back to the stack, her movement purposeful and decisive. She then turns to the chair representing the church people. "Bye," she says, her voice stronger now. "I am not going to fear your judgment." This chair, too, joins the stack.

Derrick watches all this, his gaze on the remaining chairs of his parents. "I don't know what to do," he admits.

"Try these words if they fit," I offer carefully. "If not, find your own: Tell your dad, 'you've lost everything when ma left, I feel compelled to support you in your challenges.'"

Derrick repeats the words, adding his: "I take it as a responsibility, as a filial son, to shoulder your sorrow." His eyes glisten.

"Would you be willing to sit in your father's chair?" I venture to ask. "To feel what it might be like from his perspective?"

Derrick moves hesitantly to his father's chair. His posture changes as he settles, shifting his body on it as if to feel its support. "Strange," he says, adjusting his position. His shoulders round forward, his head drops slightly—the weight of decades of mourning suddenly visible in his body. He reports feeling uncomfortable.

I ask, "As Derrick's father, what do you think your son needs to hear today?"

"I am your father." Derrick's voice is low and hoarse. "I have chosen the life I live."

Derrick and I lock eyes. Sherlyn's breath is now audible. I wait for Derrick to continue.

"I'm stuck," he says.

"Repeat after me," I say.

"Okay."

"I have chosen to mourn a woman who never loved me," I say.

"Okay," he says. He echoes my words thoughtfully, chewing on every beat. He then adds, "All I want is for you to live yours."

The words, fleshed out, come to life. They linger heavily around us. The ghost of filial obligation morphs into tenderness.

Change Happened for Sherlyn and Derrick When...

The paradoxical theory of change is poignantly depicted in Sherlyn and Derrick's journey. They didn't need techniques to overcome their intimacy barriers or strategies to manage family interference. The change process began when they stopped trying to push through their discomfort and instead gave form to what was already present—the crowded feeling of being scrutinised, the weight of others' expectations in their most private moments.

By arranging empty chairs for their invisible audience, they made the intangible tangible. This wasn't a clever intervention but a way of acknowledging what is. When Sherlyn could finally say "Leave!" to her community's chair, when Derrick could speak his truth to his father's empty seat, they weren't learning new behaviours—they were becoming more fully themselves.

Table 3.1 The Complete Paradoxical Journey

Phase	*Mei & Markus*	*Sherlyn & Derrick*	*Paradoxical Principle*
Pressure to Change	"Tell us what to do"	Three years of trying	Effort creates resistance
Resistance Encountered	Mei withdraws, Markus demands	Bodies freeze, minds worry, shame	Force increases stress
Acceptance Invitation	"What do you think you should do?"	"The people watching… let's invite them"	Honour what is present
Truth Emerges	"I am not their mother"/kids are "12-hour flight away"	"Leave!"/"I want you to live yours"	Authentic self appears
Transformation	Mei connects with her truth/Markus realises grief	Spontaneity in expression & permission to move forward where there was once inhibition	Change through awareness and being, not coercing

The phantom observers lost their power not through being ignored or overcome, but through being directly acknowledged and addressed.

Notice how change emerged organically. Sherlyn's forceful "I hate that you are all sitting here" arose from finally experiencing the full weight of this invasion, not from practising assertiveness techniques. Derrick's inability to remove his father's chair revealed the depth of his filial obligation—and in that acknowledgement, in speaking as his father saying, "All I want is for you to live yours," lay the seed of his freedom.

Both couples in this chapter came looking for solutions, yet found something more profound. The act of fully experiencing their struggles—without attempting to fix, control, or dismiss them—created space for authentic intra-psychic and inter-personal dialogue. This reflects the radical promise of the paradoxical approach: that by surrendering our desire for change, we set the stage for transformation to unfold.

The paradoxical theory of change reveals its wisdom through the complete journey of both couples—from their initial attempts to force change to their eventual discoveries through acceptance.

Conclusion

At the heart of this paradoxical wisdom lies a quality often overlooked in our outcome-focused world: curiosity. Not the intellectual curiosity that analyses and categorises, but the embodied curiosity that stays present with whatever emerges. This curiosity requires courage—the courage to resist quick fixes, to tolerate discomfort, and to trust that awareness itself holds transformative power.

For Mei and Markus, transformation came by staying with their differences long enough to uncover the grief beneath. Mei's "I am not their mother" wasn't rejection but an honouring of her own truth. Markus's recognition that his children remain "a 12-hour flight away" wasn't giving up but an acceptance of reality. In accepting what is—her need for boundaries, his sorrow over separation—they created space for a more authentic connection.

Sherlyn and Derrick's journey shows how the same principle applies to our most personal struggles. The invisible audience that had haunted their marriage for three years didn't disappear through willpower or technique. It lost its power when finally given form, when addressed directly rather than endured silently. Their courage was not in overcoming these internalised voices but in facing them, speaking to them, and ultimately reclaiming their own space.

This is what the paradoxical theory of change offers couples: not a technique or strategy, but a different way of engaging with difficulty. It encourages us to believe that within our struggles lies the potential for transformation, a wisdom, waiting not for the perfect intervention but for the right conditions—conditions of presence, acceptance, and genuine curiosity about what is.

As we've seen throughout this book—from Sarah and John rediscovering connection through decades-old music when they stopped trying to fix their distance, to Liam and Akina recognising how childhood survival strategies shaped their patterns of withdrawal, to the couples in this chapter facing cultural expectations and invisible audiences—the paradoxical principle remains constant. Whether working with trauma, navigating cultural differences, or confronting intimacy barriers, the fundamental insight endures: lasting change emerges from the courage to be more fully who we already are.

References

Beisser, A. (1970). The paradoxical theory of change. In J. Fagan & I. L. Shepherd (Eds.), *Gestalt therapy now* (pp. 77–80). Science and Behavior Books.

Perls, F. (1969/1992). *Gestalt therapy verbatim.* The Gestalt Journal Press. Kindle edition.

Yontef, G. (1992). *Awareness, dialogue and process: Essays on Gestalt therapy.* The Gestalt Journal Press.

4 The Transformative Role of Experiments in Gestalt Couples Therapy

"I pull out an empty chair and place it between us… I felt the air go dead."
—Therapist

Experiments in Gestalt Therapy

In science, we conduct experiments to study phenomena—to observe, discover, and understand what unfolds before us. These experiments require a crucible: a protected vessel strong enough to contain an exothermic chemical reaction. In Gestalt therapy, the therapy room becomes such a crucible—a safe, insulated time and space where couples can engage in trial and error without the usual consequences of their relational patterns (Hycner, 2009). Here, within clearly defined boundaries, partners can risk new ways of being together.

An experiment in Gestalt therapy springs from genuine curiosity and the desire to learn. Unlike interventions with predetermined outcomes, experiments embrace not-knowing. We ask questions rather than assume answers. We observe rather than prejudge. This distinction matters profoundly: prejudgement carries our biases, those invisible assumptions that prevent true learning. When we think we already know what will happen, we stop seeing what actually is. The experimental attitude remains radically open to whatever phenomena emerge.

The heart of experimentation lies in phenomenological observation, to see clearly what is, rather than what we expect or fear. As therapists and clients, we become phenomenological researchers, collecting data from the living laboratory of the couple's relationship. We attend to gestures, breathing patterns, voice tones, the space between bodies. We notice what emerges and what retreats, what flows and what freezes.

In Gestalt therapy, we understand experience through the lens of figure and ground. The figure describes an emerging need at any given moment—often an unfulfilled need or emotion that exists in the phenomenological field but remains outside the couple's awareness. This figure emerges from the ground—in German, "die Grund," meaning the base, the bedrock, the foundation. The ground encompasses the totality of the couple's experiences, their shared

DOI: 10.4324/9781003631545-7

history, their individual stories, and the entire life space that therapist and clients inhabit together.

The therapeutic work involves what we call "figure sharpening"—supporting the couple toward recognising and fulfilling emerging needs. The therapist senses these needs by observing phenomenological changes: a shift in posture when one partner speaks, a catch in the breath, a gesture that contradicts words. A glistening in the eyes from the ground of constant banter reveals an unspoken emerging emotion, perhaps a memory. This process brings to light the suffering or pathos that is felt by all, but often disowned or pushed aside. Importantly, this figure-ground dynamic exists within a co-created space. The suffering that exists in the therapy room is felt even before the couple enters—it permeates the atmosphere. Both therapist and clients are subjected to that something in the air, though each may make a different meaning from it. Through experiments, we sharpen these emerging figures, making tangible the feelings, emotions, and suffering that might otherwise remain ignored or overlooked. When we sharpen the figure together—when both partners can sense it, share it, witness it—transformation becomes possible.

An experiment is a creative exploration arising from the present moment between the therapist and the clients. Rather than imposing predetermined exercises, the therapist develops experiments from what already lives in the room—the couple's unique patterns, their stuck places, their yearnings. This responsiveness makes each experiment a form of improvisation, crafted for this particular couple at this particular moment.

Experiments might involve movement—switching seats to literally experience another perspective. They might use objects—rolling a ball to explore the rhythm of connection. They might work with dialogue—repeating phrases until their emotional truth emerges. Or they might embrace silence—discovering what arises when words fall away. Whatever form they take, experiments serve awareness, revealing habitual patterns and surfacing disowned feelings while opening doorways to new possibilities for contact.

The Latin root "*experiri*" simply means "to try." This trying is not about forcing change but about creating conditions where something fresh can emerge. As Zinker (1977) notes, "The experiment is the cornerstone of experiential learning. It transforms talking about into feeling and doing" (p. 123). Where traditional therapy might pursue insight through interpretation, Gestalt experiments engage the whole person—body, emotion, and spirit—awakening vitality that lies dormant within habitual patterns.

Perls, Hefferline, and Goodman (1951, pp. 278–279) introduced a powerful paradox: the "safe emergency." They recognised that genuine change requires activation—we must feel the actual tension of our stuck places. Yet this activation needs containment, a protected space where we can fully experience without being overwhelmed. The experiment creates this paradoxical state, arousing enough anxiety to mobilise change while maintaining enough safety to explore.

In this safe emergency, clients become active participants rather than passive recipients of interpretation. They immerse themselves fully—sensing, speaking, feeling, acting. The couple doesn't just talk about their distance; they experience it through positioning their chairs. They don't merely describe their pattern of pursuit and withdrawal; they embody it through movement. This full engagement transforms therapy from intellectual exercise into lived experience.

Experiments make Gestalt therapy genuinely innovative. Where most therapeutic approaches rely on interventions designed to produce specific outcomes, experiments embrace uncertainty. Innovation means changing something established, introducing new methods, creating choice where there was compulsion. When therapist and clients collaborate in experimental exploration, they enter unknown territory together.

This not-knowing is exactly what makes discovery possible. A couple trapped in repetitive conflict cannot think their way to new solutions— their thinking is part of the same pattern. But when they participate in an experiment, something unexpected may appear—a gentle gesture breaking through years of distance, a truth spoken that neither realised they possessed, a way of being together that their habitual patterns had made impossible. These discoveries come from the lived experiment itself, not from any fixed outcome.

This collaborative uncertainty—this willingness to not-know together—distinguishes Gestalt experiments from techniques that promise specific results. Throughout this book, we have witnessed the power of experiments to reveal hidden truths and create new possibilities. In Chapter 1, when John was asked to lean back and "be easy-going," it allowed him and Sarah to explore a long-forgotten connection. In Chapter 2, Liam's conversation with his father on the empty chair enabled long-buried grief to finally surface. In Chapter 3, both Sherlyn and Derrick spoke to phantoms occupying empty chairs, giving shape to the invisible presences that were disrupting their intimacy.

This chapter presents two additional case studies that further illuminate how experiments work in practice. Though the couples are fictional composites, their struggles and breakthroughs reflect real therapeutic encounters. These stories show how experiments can transform therapy from a space of problem-solving into a laboratory for creative potential.

In the first story, we meet Hai and David, a couple whose intellectual connection masks an emotional distance. Through a simple switching of seats, they discover things about themselves and each other that years of talking will never reveal. The second story features Emma and James, who, through a wordless experiment, shift from feeling separate from each other to rediscover a tenderness between them that was lost.

Experiments stem from the therapist's creativity, inspired by their attunement to the couple's emerging needs. The therapist crafts each experiment to sharpen the figure, making perceptible the needs and pathos that saturate the relational field. This is an act of "enlightening" in its purest sense: illuminating what resides in shadow, making conscious what was unconscious, transforming the unfelt into the deeply felt. Through experiments—whether switching seats, using objects, or engaging with empty chairs—couples don't just try something new—they reveal truths that years of talking could not uncover.

Case Study A: Hai and David—Walking in Your Shoes

The conversation loops stagnant in the therapy room with Hai and David exchanging grievances. My attention drifts to their feet, clad in identical white canvas sneakers—the sort one can purchase off Lazada (a Chinese online marketplace) for about fifteen dollars. "Feiyue," I absently read the blue lettering printed on them. Apart from their footwear, the men are distinct from each other in looks.

Hai and David have been discussing their upcoming wedding in Nottingham, David's hometown, where his parents and sister still reside. While this should be a joyous topic, it has become yet another arena for their differences to surface.

The soon-to-be-weds first met as students in London, where an instant connection blossomed while doing parkour with a group of fellow enthusiasts. What began as friendship evolved into a deeper relationship; they discovered love in each other and a profound understanding—a safe harbour in one another's lives.

Since relocating to Singapore, David has encountered difficulties in adapting. His professional life feels unstable and full of anxiety. "I'm trying to connect the dots. I must understand who I am in this city and how to establish myself." He describes how the move from the UK to Singapore has highlighted their differences.

At first glance, it involves David's careful, sometimes paralysing self-questioning and Hai's perpetual motion of doing.

Their current tension revolves around what David calls Hai's "gatekeeping," a pattern in which Hai controls all elements of their lives together, including household finances and David's well-being.

"Gatekeeping? I don't do that," Hai protests. "David just doesn't take care of anything in the flat or take his finances or health seriously. He just waits for me to think about everything."

"Oh gosh, I don't need you to do all my thinking for me, Hai," David replies. "And I'm fine on my own; I'm not in any trouble." He slaps both hands down on his lap.

I enjoy their back-and-forth. In their banter, frustration lies beneath the surface, but a deep affection shines through. Their ongoing argument transports me back to my childhood when mostly young boys in the neighbourhood would play "sepak takraw" each evening. It is a game of striking a rattan ball with the feet and passing it over a net. The neighbourhood kids demonstrate their self-taught dexterity in fierce competition. From the flats above, we would hear their multilingual exclamations, such as "*wa liao*!" and "*alamak*!" before erupting into laughter.

I lose myself in silence. They turn their attention towards me. In the spirit of play, I suggest, "Let's try something!"

"Oh!" They say in unison.

"It is not dangerous," is my assurance. The guys respond with a giggly laughter.

I ask them to take a moment to observe each other closely and to notice how the person across from them carried himself—the angle of his posture, the placement of his arms and legs, and the expressions that danced across his face.

David and Hai breathe instinctively in unison. They pause, waiting for a nod from each other before rising from their seats, shuffling their matching white trainers across the carpet. A collective giggle ensues as they switch places.

"Awesome," I say, watching them settle into each other's places.

"Now," I add, "lower your gaze and picture yourself as the person who occupied this chair. Hai, you are now David. David, you are now Hai. Feel into your body what it is like to be each other. What does it feel like to be in his body? Notice the tensions, the impulses."

They quietly embrace their new roles, their bodies subtly transforming as if trying on new skins. When I asked them to look at one another, their gazes were no longer the same as before.

Turning to David, who is in Hai's chair, I ask, "What do you feel in your body right now, Hai?"

David closes his eyes as if to absorb my question. "As Hai, I feel the need to be strong. I need to be vigilant," his voice dropping to almost a whisper. "I'm feeling tense—my shoulder aches. I'm tired." He twists his shoulders as if to loosen its stiffness. He pauses mid-movement. "I feel…alone." The last word is like a confession.

"I sense a deep solitude as I see you in this chair." I say, "I'm wondering if you can say what you need from David?"

The person in the opposite chair nods silently.

David pauses, his face softening as he searches for words. "I need you to see me," he says finally, surprise colouring his voice. "I don't know why I'm saying this, but it feels right to say, 'I need you to see me.'"

Hai speaks from David's chair, his words rushing, "As David, I feel strangely unclear, lost, messy, small. I don't know what my role is. My stomach is rumbling." His voice cracks. "Yet I feel the deep need to be noticed, to matter. I feel left alone."

The room is silent. David yawns.

"Something making you sleepy?" I ask.

"Yes," David responds through another yawn. "I feel an exhaustion. I've been exhausted all this while."

The men exchange a few more rounds of words. Like the faithful retreating to their pews, their movement is measured and reverent; they return to their original seats, symbolising a return to themselves. A collective exhale resonates, releasing tension as they sink back into familiarity.

David remains caught up in yawns. Hai's giggle drifts softly in the stillness.

"I feel really awkward," says David.

Hai leans forward, "Are you okay, David?"

"I don't like what I see." David's voice cracks.

I ask him what he sees.

"I dislike how I am perceived, as someone lacking clarity, someone uncertain."

I check with him to see which part of Hai's reflection affects him.

"But what Hai said is right," David admits.

"It is not comfortable being seen?" I ask.

They nod in unison.

"What, if anything, do you need…from either of us now, David?" I ask.

David yawns again, "Hmm."

"I love you so much," Hai interjects. "I felt seen when you took my seat and spoke as if you were me."

He explains how he experienced sadness as well.

"And I feel a tinge of loneliness, hearing your words," I say.

"That is funny," David admits, wiping a trace of tears from his eyes. "I have craved all my life to be seen, and yet being seen is so difficult, so utterly painful."

Hai learned from a young age to be "the good child" and the responsible one in a household where his father was mostly absent and his mother's anger could erupt without notice. Each perfect action was a shield against the lash of her bamboo cane, and every responsibility he took was a safeguard against disorder. He taught himself to be on his guard without anyone else to defend him and to do everything himself.

David's life began with a congenital illness that transformed his mother's love into an obsessive force. Her concern manifested in endless cleaning, constant medical vigilance, and a home so pristine that traces of David's existence there felt like a transgression. His childhood bedroom was the only space he could exist without causing his mother more work and worry—sanctuary and prison—the rest of the house linked to her compulsive need for control. "Mum was the gatekeeper par excellence."

As the session comes to an end, their bickering fades from memory. In its void lies an acknowledgement, a deeper understanding. Similar to the *sepak takraw* players in my neighbourhood who have since grown up, their game continues to evolve.

What the Experiment Revealed

The role reversal experiment bypassed Hai and David's intellectual defences, accessing the body's wisdom that exists beneath conscious awareness. When David inhabited Hai's physical posture, he didn't just understand Hai's exhaustion intellectually; he felt the loneliness of constant vigilance in his own muscles and bones. Similarly, when Hai experienced David's position, he encountered the profound discomfort of being seen—"I don't like what I see," David later admitted, his voice cracking with unacknowledged shame.

These figures—loneliness and shame—had been hidden beneath their surface bickering about gatekeeping and finances. The experiment sharpened these obscured emotions, bringing them to light. David's whispered "I need you to see me" carried the shame of feeling invisible, while his later confession—"I have craved all my life to be seen, and yet being seen is so difficult, so utterly painful"—revealed how shame and longing intertwine. Through feeling and sharing these vulnerable emotions rather than defending against them, the men found compassion and connection.

Yet not all couples arrive with such capacity for playful exploration. Our next story presents a more fundamental challenge: what happens when withdrawal has become so entrenched that experimentation itself seems impossible? Emma and James demonstrate how even the simplest gesture can become revolutionary when absence, rather than conflict, organises the relational field.

Case Study B: Emma and James—When Nobody's Home

James arrives first, settling into the armchair with the air of someone resigned and anticipating disappointment. "Emma's probably still at work," he says, more to himself than to me.

While we wait, James methodically fills out the intake form, explaining their situation efficiently: Eight years of marriage, two boys aged four and eight. A colleague—one of my former clients—had recommended they try couples' therapy. "Why not," he says with a hollow laugh. "We have nothing more to lose."

Emma finally enters the room ten minutes late; her presence announcing itself before she does—the tapping of stilettos and perfume that dominates the space around us. Her knit dress flows around her curves as she moves to the sofa across from James. Her eyes skim past him as he gazes firmly at the carpet—the physical distance between them is a chasm.

"Do I really have to fill this out?" she asks, glancing at the intake form, barely concealing irritation. Completing it with sharp, quick ink strokes, she looks up. "And now what?"

The silence that follows her question feels charged with something I can't quite name—not tension, but a sterile emptiness.

"*Is this what home feels like?*" I address the carpet.

James clears his throat, "It's hardly ever this quiet at home. Not with our boys."

He vividly describes their home routine—chaotic mornings as the children argue over socks and toothbrushing, their domestic helper struggling to maintain order, and mealtimes that become battlegrounds over food preferences. But beneath the noise and activity he describes, I sense a more resounding silence—the quiet of parents moving through their days like ghosts, speaking through their children.

As James speaks, Emma's fingers drum a rhythm of triplets on the armrest. "Of course, the children only listen to him," she interjects sharply. "My plans always get thwarted. I might as well not be there."

"And where would you go when you're not 'there'?" I ask.

Emma describes her evenings out—dinners with colleagues, spa appointments, night courses—a separate life carefully constructed. She cuts in again, "He's not even there either. It's dinner at his mother's with the boys every night."

James's silence communicates volumes. I sense a pull into a pattern of losing myself. The questions I long to ask them—why they are here and what they hope to gain from this session—stay unvoiced.

Their constructed separateness becomes increasingly intense as the session unfolds. Each has skilfully carved out an escape route from the emptiness at home: Emma to her "extracurricular activities" and James to his mother's house. I find myself drawn to the role of a messenger, who, perhaps like their children, is spoken through to connect the two. I wander silently in the standoff, observing Emma and James drift apart into separate spaces—the screaming void pounds at my eardrums.

Following a familiar instinct, I pull out an empty chair and place it between us. "Let's imagine that your relationship occupies this chair," I recite, yet the oppressive stillness in the room only deepens as we stare dumbfounded at the vacant seat. I felt the air go dead. Emma (whose eyes had turned glassy) and James silently gaze at the floor. The emptiness of the chair intensifies the void between them, chanting a resounding, "No, no!" in the silence. I realise we're trying to perceive nothing with nothing. The task feels as hollow as the space we're attempting to engage with. The empty chair sat between us, somehow amplifying rather than bridging their disconnect. I noticed Emma's body subtly angling away, her crossed arms tightening. James's jaw clenched, his breathing shallow. The air itself seemed to recoil. This wasn't resistance to be overcome—it was vital information.

"Oh well, it seems this isn't a good idea," I said, putting the chair back on its stack. I am now drawn to the rarely used, oversized, inflated exercise ball in the corner. In my boredom, such an object can seem like a refreshing addition. I roll it towards our chairs, gliding across the carpet towards James.

His hand reaches out automatically, fingers giving it a gentle flick that sends it moving toward Emma. There's a fleeting spark of playfulness in his gesture.

The ball bumps softly against Emma's shin. "Tsk!" The sound escapes her lips like a reflex, sharp with irritation as if we're children interrupting her adult business. She lets the ball roll away, her slight recoil visible in how her body shifts back in her chair.

The brief flicker in Jamess eyes extinguishes, and his shoulders droop slightly.

"Your expression changed," I say to James.

He sits with this observation, his hands now stiffly on his lap. Clearing his throat again, "I feel a sadness," his voice carries a weight that seems to sink into the carpet.

"What if you said this directly to Emma?"

He turns toward her, eyes not meeting hers. "I feel a sadness."

"Try again," I encourage. "Say it more personally."

This time, he says, "Emma, I feel sad."

"I hear what you're saying," she responds, her tone carrying years of what sounds like practised defence. "But it's been too long."

"What did you experience when the ball touched you?" I ask Emma.

Her answer spills out with unexpected force: "It's too late. There's nothing there. Nothing left." She straightens her dress with sharp movements. 2I feel no love from him. He and the boys—they don't even want me around. What's the point of being there when nobody listens to me?"

"What makes Emma feel that she is so unlikable, you reckon?" I ask, making an inverted comma gesture with my hands at the word "unlikeable."

"She nags," he replies without a thought.

"I don't like things they do, their eating habits." Her tone reminds me of my nit-picky primary school Chinese language teacher. "James and the boys are in cahoots with each other. The boys fight to sit with him on the bus, at restaurants, and even on planes. Never with me."

"Yes, that's how it is," James says quietly, his foot nudging absently at the ball. "But it feels like we can't do anything right."

"And no one cares to listen to me." The words escape Emma.

"What does that mean for you when they disregard your opinion?"

"It means I'm redundant. Deselected. Not chosen." Each word from her is precise, "So I spend time away. I'm just making real what's already true."

The ball rests between them, a silent witness. James looks at it, then at Emma, as if seeing her clearly for the first time. "I take the boys to my mother's because..." he starts, then stops. "Because at least there, someone wants us around."

Their parallel retreats are apparent.

"When James tried to make contact with you through the ball just now," I ask, "what did you sense?"

"He's doing it only because you are here," Emma replies quickly, emphasising the word "you." "After all, it's therapy protocol."

"Therapy protocol would actually look like this," I reply, "I would ask if you'd like to try this..." Gently, I tap the ball into a slight bounce. "Feel the bounce in your palms as you send and receive it."

James moves first, his touch tentative as he guides the ball toward Emma. The ball rolls smoothly across the short distance between them. Emma's hand reaches out—not pushing it away this time, but catching it and holding it for a moment before sending it back.

They maintain this silent exchange, each roll becoming increasingly fluid. No words are exchanged between them. The ball moves back and forth, pendulating.

As the ball rolls into the space between them, I feel suddenly lighter, as if it is gracefully taking my place. Where I had been straining to bridge their disconnection—tempted to become the messenger between two isolated worlds the ball now carries that function wordlessly. My body relaxes, no longer needing to hold the tension of their separation. The ball is now the fourth presence in the room, neutral and patient, allowing me to return to my position as witness rather than bridge.

The ball appears to convey a wordless dialogue.

Delighting in the moment, I lose touch with time. I momentarily forget the time—perhaps minutes, perhaps longer. The rhythmic back-and-forth seems to exist outside ordinary temporality. Then I notice the couple heave a combined sigh of relief, their shoulders dropping in unison. I realise at that moment that we are breathing, which means that we haven't been before this.

In the ensuing weeks, subtle, barely noticeable changes emerge in their sessions. Emma accepted the challenge of establishing a nook at home that is just hers—a rug, cushions, and a small table for her hobby, miniature painting. It's a modest setup, just a few square feet in the living room of their three-bedroom apartment that belongs to her exclusively, a space where only she ruled and she would not feel "harassed" by the kids. Its existence alters the dynamics of the house. The boys, who were initially told not to disturb their mum's space, began to take an interest in it, often obediently sitting at its perimeter.

James finds himself lingering at home more often, and his nightly retreats to his mother's house are becoming less frequent. "The boys asked to stay home yesterday," he tells me during one session.

We never speak directly about what's shifting between them. There are no dramatic declarations, no grand gestures of reconciliation. Instead, Emma now chooses to read in her corner rather than schedule another facial appointment. James is bringing home a better lamp for her space. There's the gradual filling of the void between them with small, ordinary moments of being at home.

In our final session together, the exercise ball makes one last appearance. As they roll it between them, their movements have the ease of practice, of something learned and relearned until it becomes natural. No one has told Emma she isn't redundant. No one has assured James that his presence is valued. But here they are, sending these truths back and forth between them in the simple physics of an inflated ball.

"What's different now?" I ask.

Emma's hand rests on the ball. "The house feels more like home," she says simply. James nods, his hand joining hers on the curved surface between them.

What the Experiment Revealed

Emma and James's session demonstrates how experiments need not be elaborate to be transformative. The crucial experiment occurred when the therapist asked James to speak directly to Emma about his feeling of sadness. This simple redirection disrupted their habitual pattern of communicating through third parties—be it their children, the helper, parents, or even the therapist. By suppressing their usual triangulated communication and requiring direct address, genuine dialogue became possible for the first time.

The failed empty chair experiment provided equally valuable information. The couple's inability to imagine their relationship as a presence revealed the depth of absence organising their field. This "failure" guided the therapist toward something more basic—the exercise ball that could carry connection without requiring them to conceptualise what they'd lost. Through this wordless exchange, their bodies remembered a rhythm of send-and-receive that their words could no longer access.

What emerged was not dramatic reconciliation but something quieter: Emma creating a small corner just for herself, James lingering at home more often. The experiments revealed that beneath their elaborate parallel lives lay a simple truth—they had forgotten how to occupy the same space. By practicing direct communication and physical exchange, they began relearning the fundamental grammar of connection.

These varied experiments—from verbal redirection to embodied play—illustrate how therapeutic creativity must respond to each couple's unique field. To understand how experiments work at deeper levels, we turn now to Claudio Naranjo's framework, which illuminates the dual mechanisms through which experimental work creates change.

Two Ways Experiments Work: Naranjo's Lens

Gestalt experiments don't follow a single formula—they serve different purposes depending on the couple and the moment. As Claudio Naranjo (1993) observed, experiments can be:

- **Suppressive** These help pause or interrupt a familiar pattern. By momentarily holding back a habitual reaction (like blame, withdrawal, or control), space opens for something new or hidden to surface.
  Example: Hai stepping into David's shoes disrupted their usual blame dynamic and made space for grief to emerge.
- **Expressive** These invite something unspoken or disowned into the room. They give voice—or movement, or sound—to aspects of self or relationship that have been held in.
  Example: Emma and James using the exercise ball allowed a wordless tenderness to surface that language had shut down.

Both types support awareness and contact. What matters is that they arise from the therapist's creativity through attuned sensing, not from protocol.

Understanding Experiments Through Practice

While Naranjo's distinction between suppressive and expressive techniques provides a theoretical framework, the true art lies in recognising how these approaches manifest in the living moment of therapy.

When to Experiment—and When Not To

While experiments can powerfully transform stuck patterns, they emerge best from a grounded, confident, therapeutic presence. The therapist's own state profoundly influences whether an experiment serves or harms. When we feel rushed, stressed, or uncertain, our experiments tend to become forced interventions rather than creative explorations. In these moments, less is more—staying with simple presence often serves couples better than elaborate experiments.

The field itself usually signals when experimental work isn't appropriate. When active violence or severe power imbalances dominate a relationship, experiments risk reinforcing harmful dynamics rather than transforming them. Similarly, when trust has been shattered, perhaps through recent betrayal or deception, the wound needs gentle tending before playful exploration becomes possible. Acute intoxication, severe dissociation, or active psychosis create fields where reality itself feels unstable, making experimental work potentially overwhelming rather than illuminating.

Cultural context shapes how we offer experiments, requiring us to sense beyond our own familiar frameworks. In some cultural contexts, building relational trust through many sessions of talking precedes any invitation to embodied work. What might seem like resistance could be cultural wisdom about pacing and propriety. A therapist grounded in their own body can usually sense these cultural rhythms—feeling when an experiment would violate unspoken boundaries versus when it might open new possibilities.

The beauty of experimental work lies in its flexibility. Couples themselves often modify experiments to fit their comfort level, and this modification itself becomes valuable information. When a couple from a culture that values emotional restraint finds switching seats too exposing, perhaps they begin by simply noticing their postures, or imagining what sitting differently might feel like. The experiment adapts to honour their boundaries while still inviting awareness.

Sometimes the most therapeutic act is recognising when not to experiment at all. A grounded therapist trusts this recognition, knowing that presence itself—being fully there with a couple in their struggle—creates its own transformative potential. When we're centred and confident, we can sense whether the field calls for creative experimentation or simple witnessing. When we're depleted or activated ourselves, honouring our limitations by keeping things simple often serves everyone best. The principle remains: experiments arise from abundance and presence, not from anxiety about "doing something." In this way, even our restraint becomes a form of therapeutic wisdom.

Conclusion: The Transformative Power of Experimental Work

Experiments in Gestalt couples therapy are co-created events—emergent, alive, and grounded in the immediacy of the therapeutic situation. They shift the process from talking about problems to being with what is, bringing submerged emotions and needs from ground to figure where they can finally be acknowledged. Something begins to stir when partners step out of familiar positions and into shared presence.

In Hai and David's session, the role reversal experiment suppressed their habitual banter, allowing the emotions beneath—loneliness and shame—to surface. For Emma and James, the experiments suppressed their pattern of living as isolated individuals, beginning with the simple act of James telling Emma directly, "I feel sad." Their wordless ball exchange then allowed connection to flow where words had failed. These experiments didn't solve their problems but shed light on what lay hidden, creating conditions for genuine contact.

Experimentation in therapy is not about intervention or collecting tools. The empty chair, perhaps Gestalt's most recognised yet misunderstood element, exemplifies this confusion. When therapists mechanically place chairs without phenomenological attunement—without sensing what wants to emerge—they reduce a living process to dead technique. Fritz Perls was clear: techniques are "gimmicks," that "(i)n Gestalt therapy, we are working for something else. We are here to promote the growth process and to develop the human potential" (Perls, 1969, p. 16). The chair means nothing without the therapist's presence, without feeling into the field's rhythm and noticing what movements might invite discovery.

True experimental work first requires phenomenological attunement—sensing the field's qualities, the couple's readiness, and the emerging figures. From this attunement, experiments arise organically. They facilitate contact by revealing what interrupts it. When couples can't complete an experiment, we don't push harder—we become curious about the interruption itself. What makes switching seats impossible? Why does direct communication feel dangerous? These interruptions often point precisely toward what needs attention.

All therapy grounded in curiosity and attention is inherently experimental. The therapy room as crucible implies this spirit of discovery. When clients request homework or exercises, hoping for concrete solutions, we might respond with gentle honesty: "Life is difficult enough already without adding more tasks. Instead, let's experiment here together—try things out and see what emerges. If something doesn't work, we'll explore what interrupts it."

This experimental attitude embodies the paradoxical theory of change—not trying to fix or force, but staying present with what is until it transforms from within. We thrive in not-knowing, following what emerges, letting emotions surface in their own time. This is the essence of Gestalt therapy: not a collection of techniques but a way of being with couples that trusts in awareness itself as the catalyst for change.

As we turn to the next chapter, we expand our view from these intimate experiments to the larger forces at play. Field theory reveals how individual struggles emerge from broader contexts—cultural expectations, family histories, and invisible loyalties that shape every interaction. If experiments show us how change happens in the moment, field theory illuminates why certain patterns persist and what larger forces must be acknowledged for transformation to take root.

References

Hycner, R. (2009). *Relational approaches in Gestalt therapy*. Gestalt Press.
Naranjo, C. (1993). *Gestalt therapy: The attitude and practice of an atheoretical experientialism*. Gateways/Arica Institute.
Perls, F., Hefferline, R. F., & Goodman, P. (1951). *Gestalt therapy: Excitement and growth in the human personality*. Julian Press.
Perls, F. S. (1969). *Gestalt therapy verbatim*. Real People Press.
Zinker, J. (1977). *Creative process in Gestalt therapy*. Brunner/Mazel.

Part III

The Field and Connection

5 Field Theory in Couples Therapy

> "I, too, am wrapped in a velvet robe, one woven from the expectations of others."
>
> —Siya

The Therapy Room Shifts

The air thickens before she speaks. I feel a heaviness in the room that wasn't there moments ago. Her fingers trace the edge of her smartphone over and over, a hypnotic rhythm that pulls my attention. The empty chair beside her seems to breathe, to pulse with presence. "He's not coming," she finally says, "I suppose you already know." The knowing arrived before her words, carried on the atmosphere itself.

This is how the field announces itself: not through analysis or observation, but through the body's immediate recognition. Before I can name what's happening, I'm already a part of it. The loneliness that fills this room isn't just hers; it has become ours, reshaping the therapeutic space into something dense.

This is field theory in action, a lived reality that shapes every moment of couples therapy.

When couples seek our help, they often request solutions for "fixing their communication" or "stopping their arguments." Yet these visible struggles arise from invisible forces—the field that holds and shapes their relationship. What if, instead of immediately trying to solve these problems, we first learned to sense the larger patterns at play? How can we understand how the therapist's willingness to feel the weight of absence and the texture of disconnection is inherently therapeutic?

Field theory transforms the way we understand suffering in relationships. Rather than locating problems inside individuals—"he drinks too much," "she's too critical"—we begin to perceive how pain emerges also from the spaces between people, from the invisible threads of history, culture, and expectation that bind them. This shift from individual pathology to field phenomena doesn't just change our theories; it changes what becomes possible in the therapy room.

DOI: 10.4324/9781003631545-9

Understanding "Field"

Imagine dropping a stone into still water. The ripples extend outward, each affecting the next, creating patterns that couldn't exist without the whole. This is how field theory understands relationships—not as two separate individuals who happen to interact, but as an inseparable web of influences where everything affects everything else.

Kurt Lewin (1951), who pioneered field theory, captured it in a deceptively simple formula: **Life Space = Person + Environment**, where the field is the life space (Staemmler, 2006). But this mathematical expression contains a radical insight: we cannot understand a person separate from their world, nor can we grasp an environment without considering how it exists for that particular person. Your partner's mood shifts the atmosphere. Your childhood experiences colour how you hear their words. The therapist's presence changes what can be spoken. Everything connects.

Perls, Hefferline, & Goodman (1951) as founders of Gestalt therapy, took Lewin's insight into the therapeutic profession and recognised how the individual—the organism (Goldstein, 1939)— is integral to the environment. This interaction of the organism and environment is termed the "organism/environment field" (p. 4). For brevity in this book, we will use the term "field" to mean the "organism/environment field." The individual and their world are one continuous process, meeting and shaping each other at every moment. We use "being of the field" rather than describing the individual as being in the field.

A Field Theory Reconceptualisation of the Therapist's Position

Field theory fundamentally transforms our understanding of the therapeutic encounter, distinguishing the Gestalt approach from traditional therapeutic modalities. Unlike conventional frameworks where therapists position themselves as external observers—akin to scientists studying specimens through a microscope—field theory recognises that therapists are irreducibly part of the therapeutic field. We don't merely observe the couple's dynamics from a safe distance; we are immersed within it, shaped by it, and simultaneously shaping it through our response (Parlett 1991; Perls et al. 1951; Philippson, 2009).

Traditional mono-personal approaches in psychopathology focus on identifying problems within individuals, such as depression, anxiety, or personality disorders, as if these issues exist independently within the person. The therapist acts as if they were external experts, addressing the client's internal pathology as an observer. Bi-personal perspectives have expanded this view by emphasising the importance of the therapeutic relationship itself, exploring transference, countertransference, and the working alliance. However, even this dyadic focus overlooks an important aspect.

Field theory goes beyond just recognising limitations by understanding that the therapeutic situation involves much more than individual minds or even the therapist–client relationship. The field constitutes the holistic organisation of the therapeutic setting, where all participants—therapist and clients—are in contact with and passively influenced by everything occurring in the here and now of the session. This includes the room's atmosphere, cultural forces, family histories lurking invisibly, the city lights visible through the window, and even the empty chair that "speaks." This lived experience is typically emergent, unique, fleeting, situated, co-created, corporeal, and ever-changing (Francesetti, 2015 & 2019).

These theoretical foundations—the organism/environment field, the therapist as participant rather than observer—come alive through the lived experience of therapy. In the following story, we'll witness how field forces announce themselves from the first moments of contact: in the quality of absence that fills a room, in the weight of cultural expectations that shape every gesture, in the invisible threads that bind across generations. Siya and Sam's relationship exists within a complex web of influences—religious traditions, family loyalties, economic reversals, and intergenerational patterns—that create their unique relational field. As you read their story—(which is written in two parts, in this chapter and Chapter 8— notice how the field informs through immediate, embodied experience: the scent of perfume masking absence, the empty chair that somehow breathes with presence, the spontaneous emergence of metaphors that capture what literal language cannot.

Siya and Sam

Siya's fingers drum against her smartphone screen. The blue ticks are telling her that he has read her messages. He doesn't reply to them. The woody scent of her perfume permeates the room, standing in for her husband's absence.

Sam's empty chair speaks. He agreed to join today's session, and he texted an hour ago to excuse himself. He says, once again, he's attending a late evening client meeting. The familiar pattern of their relationship plays out in their sessions—his absence, her waiting. She apologises on his behalf.

"Last night, I waited till nine-thirty. Priya was hungry and wouldn't eat. She insisted on waiting for her papa, but the food was getting cold. Even Pepper"—she smiles slightly at the mention of their miniature schnauzer—"kept running to the door every time he heard footsteps in the corridor."

It's now 7:15 pm. Siya's work schedule makes it impossible for her to attend therapy earlier in the day. The financial district of Singapore, visible from my window, shines with its nightly glow. Siya presumes that Sam is one of the many still working in one of those towers. This evening, Little Priya is at home having food with their domestic helper, and Pepper waits at the door.

"So, when did you finally get to eat?" I ask.

"I fed Priya first. She has to get up early for school tomorrow. Then I just had some chips. I completely lost my appetite." She tilts her head and drops her gaze to her hands on her lap.

At work, Siya handles major cases and is on track to be a partner at the firm. "Today I was in court till four, then back-to-back client calls till six." She adds matter-of-factly, "And I still made it home to check on Priya before coming over."

"He works as a financial advisor," she continues. "These late nights are about entertaining clients to close deals, but I see all the credit card statements. The bar tabs, all drinks."

"What do those bar tabs mean to you, Siya?"

"He drinks too much," she says, "but when I confront him, he says that he needs to entertain clients to sell the policies." She laughs bitterly. "He sells barely enough to pay for his golf membership."

The bar tabs repeat the story echoing generations: that Sam's father drank and "womanised"—a word we strangely hardly use today, was a sore point in his family. "I earn five times his salary. I pay the mortgage, Priya's school fees, and even his car instalments."

"I feel a heaviness within me hearing you," I say. There are questions swirling in my mind. I save them for later.

"I cannot say this to anyone. But I cannot do this anymore. I don't know why I'm still doing this. I feel so alone."

"We met because our parents had 'arranged' it," she says, gesturing with her hands in the air as if to signify quotation marks. Marrying someone chosen by one's parents has been a non-obligatory practice in her family for a generation. Her parents met each other at their workplace. "I had just finished my A levels, and Sam had just completed National Service. Our parents met at a common friend's wedding and came up with the idea to match us. We belonged to the same religious sect, good families…it was perfect, on paper."

"My parents are also lawyers. There was never any question that I would study law. All my cousins were doctors and lawyers," she says, her voice trailing off. "But there was always this other expectation, too…that I would be properly married to someone suitable, who carries the same religious values, and approved by my family."

That child who comes up with the goods.

"His family had money. At least they set aside money to take him, their only son, to an Ivy League school in the US after his National Service. Everyone was saying to me, Si, you are so lucky." She lets out a bitter laugh. "Nobody outside the family was supposed to know that he dropped out."

And by then, everything was set in motion.

"I thought he could make up for it by working in insurance," her voice tight. "Most of my friends in the industry are in the 'Million Dollar Round Table'."

And they don't need drinks to close their deals.

She had reservations early on. "I was interning at the law firm. But his mother… She treated him like he was made of some precious metal and bestowed on him a velvet robe. His father was never at home. Sam used to tell me how he would hear his mother wail and weep over his father's infidelities. She had no one to turn to but her son. She would tell Sam everything on her mind, and she still does."

Since their wedding, Siya has felt diminished by her mother-in-law's comments, particularly when others are around. Her mother-in-law is deeply religious, and her faith has influenced how she raised her son. She showered Sam with protective love, making him special, above criticism, the focus of her world. What started as a way to shield him became a pattern that neither of them benefited from in his adult relationships. For many, this devotion symbolised love, protection, and a sense of hope for the future. Mothers often invest heavily in their sons, viewing them as a safeguard for the future and a means of upholding family honour. However, without proper boundaries, even the strongest love can become stifling.

"But I made one thing clear to Sam before we married," her voice sharp. "I told him that coming home drunk was a deal breaker. I told him that would be absolutely non-negotiable."

Siya grew up listening to her father's carefully chosen stories— each one a lesson wrapped in metaphor. He was a man who grew up surrounded by older sisters. He witnessed their gradual diminishment under the weight of financial dependency on their husbands and controlling mothers-in-law. Their struggles left an indelible mark on his approach to raising his daughter.

His fatherly bedtime stories included ancient fables, carefully selecting those that emphasised wisdom and self-reliance. His favourite metaphor, echoing through Siya's adult years, compared marriage to fishing: "When looking for fish," he would tell her, "never settle for a canal when the open sea awaits."

I recall with fondness my late father saying the same thing four decades ago, but in a different language.

Siya swallows hard, "And yet, here I am, cleaning Sam's vomit off our living room floor."

Oh! I'd be outta here! I say in silence.

"Last month, I moved into the guest room," she confesses.

While he sleeps in the master room of the apartment she pays for.

"Then his mother called to say I was selfish and that a good wife stays by her husband's side no matter what."

Oh.

"But what am I teaching my daughter by staying?"

A tough call indeed.

"The hardest part isn't even the judgement from others," she says. "It's the guilt I feel. Like I'm betraying everyone, my parents, our community, even his mother. But I'm also betraying myself by staying. And Priya..."

"I see her watching me, taking everything in," Siya says, her voice softening when speaking of her daughter. "Last week, Priya found me crying at my computer during a late work night. She sat with me and said, 'It's only work, Mama,' she said. She's only six, but she is already so insightful."

Siya straightens in her chair. "She had been sneaking packets of her favourite biscuits into my laptop bag. When I asked her why, she said it was for me, 'in case you forget to eat lunch again, Mama.' The way she watches over me…"

Tears in my eyes threaten to trickle down my cheeks. I do not try to hide them.

Siya's voice trails off, with the weight of acknowledging the reversed roles. "A child shouldn't have to worry about her mother's eating habits or emotional state," she raises her hands, in a prayer position, to her lips. "I'm in therapy because I am seeing how my struggles affect her. It's wrong. I am not going to become my mother-in-law."

"I want her to have movie nights and bedtime stories, not worry about whether her mother is eating or her father is drinking. But leaving…" She swallows hard. "Leaving means I'd be the one breaking up her family. How can I ever forgive myself for that?"

Siya's sessions often had me speaking more to myself than to her. Sam would make sporadic appearances in the subsequent sessions. He embodies a golden child ensnared in his mother's velvet devotional robe. I have come to understand how this garment both adorns and suffocates. His time in America had provided him with a taste of freedom from deification, but he had spiralled without the skills to manage such liberty. Now, that same pattern threatens everything—his marriage, his relationship with Priya, and his sense of self.

When Sam does appear in therapy, his presence mirrors the same patterns that play out at home. He arrives late, full of elaborate explanations about client meetings and market conditions. His charm, honed through years of deflecting his mother's concerns, fills the room like a familiar cologne—sweet but ultimately cloying. But he insists, "I'm not drinking that much. Siya exaggerates everything. She's the one threatening to break up our family. What kind of mother does that to her child?" Each time he shows up, it's with the same script—minimizing his drinking, shifting blame to Siya's "unkindness," positioning himself as the victim of her "unreasonable standards." During these sessions, I see the helplessness in his eyes. I am also acutely aware of his tendency for violent outbursts when his issues are not given precedence.

But Sam is not the child in this family.

Every small act of autonomy—moving to the guest room, voicing concerns about drinking, attending therapy independently—grants Siya a quiet liberation. Establishing boundaries at home, no longer tolerating his no-shows and tantrums, and making personal decisions independently without seeking approval from her in-laws are immensely challenging endeavours for her.

"I am overwhelmed with guilt," she admits each time she tries to reach a modest milestone. "However, it's becoming increasingly less powerful than my desire to demonstrate a different way of being a woman to my daughter."

Respect for tradition and self-preservation aren't necessarily mutually exclusive.

Siya gathers her belongings at the end of our session in the dimming light of my office. Her shoulders squared to face yet another evening. She pauses at the doorway, her silhouette backlit by the corridor lights. "Sometimes I think I, too, am wrapped in a velvet robe," she reflects. "One woven from the expectations of others."

"Robes that are bestowed need not be worn forever," I say as we leave the building. "Have a good night, Siya."

As she melds with the city's glow, I see a woman in transition.

Field Dynamics in Siya and Sam's Story

Through Siya and Sam's session, we witness how field theory principles manifest in lived therapeutic experience. The atmosphere transforms from the opening moments—Siya's dutifulness in arriving on time while apologising for Sam's absence reveals patterns far deeper than individual behaviour. These relational dynamics express cultural forces about gender roles and obligations, speaking through their bodies, timing, and positioning in space.

The therapist's experience of heaviness demonstrates field contemporaneity—how past and future collapse into the present moment. Siya's exhaustion carries the accumulated weight of her entire existence, not merely today's disappointments. When the therapist chooses to withhold questions and stay with silence, she engages with the field's pathos, its essential suffering that becomes palpable in the therapeutic space. This is how everything that matters exists right now in this moment of contact.

The velvet robe emerges as a natural metaphor from the therapeutic relationship itself, capturing what literal language cannot. Such spontaneous images reveal the field's aesthetic dimension, communicating meaning through resonance and shared understanding. Similarly, when Siya's father's wisdom about "fishing in the open sea" bridges cultures and generations, we see how the field creates its own language of connection.

Throughout the session, nothing proves irrelevant. Sam's patterns of absence and blame-shifting actively shape the field, while the therapist's unexpressed emotions—sadness, helplessness, even anger—become qualities of the field itself. Even her realisation that she speaks less with Siya reveals field dynamics: "perhaps Siya needs space to hear her own voice after years of silence." In field theory, silence itself speaks, and every phenomenon carries potential meaning for understanding the couple's unique relational world.

The therapist's experience throughout this session reveals how we are not external observers but active participants in the field. Every sensation, emotion, and impulse provide valuable information about the couple's "life space".

Sam's relationship with his mother illustrates how individual patterns emerge from larger cultural and evolutionary contexts. This pattern—mothers

Table 5.1 The Therapist is "of the Field"

Therapist's Experience	*What It Reveals About the Field*	*How It Informs the Work*
Feeling heaviness before Siya speaks	The field's pathos is palpable, announces itself atmospherically	Alerts therapist to depth of suffering before words are spoken
"Oh! I'd be outta here!" (silent reaction)	Visceral response to cleaning vomit—field's exhaustion enters therapist	Validates Siya's experience through shared embodied reaction
Tears threatening when hearing about Priya	Child's reversed caretaking role evokes universal protective response	Strengthens therapeutic alliance through authentic emotional presence
Speaking less with Siya than other clients	Field organised around Siya's need to find her own voice	Therapist intuitively provides space rather than filling it
Noticing the empty chair "breathing"	Sam's absence has presence; the field includes those not physically there	Recognises how absence shapes the field as powerfully as presence

turning to sons for emotional sustenance—appears across cultures and throughout history. Freud (1917) noted how maternal favouritism creates both confidence and burden in men. What once served evolutionary purposes—mothers investing in sons as future protectors—now requires conscious navigation in modern relationships where emotional intimacy with partners becomes possible. In field theory terms, Sam's "velvet robe" represents not just his family's specific dynamics but a universal human pattern that manifests differently across cultural contexts.

To understand these field dynamics more deeply, we can turn to Malcolm Parlett's (1991) articulation of field theory through five organising principles. Having witnessed these principles in action through Siya and Sam's session, we can now examine how they provide a framework for understanding the therapeutic field.

Parlett's Five Principles: Understanding Field Dynamics

Parlett's (1991) articulation of field theory through five principles offers a framework for understanding Gestalt therapy's field theory:

Principle 1: **Organisation** Fields are organised wholes where meaning derives from analysing the entire context, including all existing facts. This principle encourages us to go beyond examining isolated elements and to understand how all parts of a field are interconnected and influence each other. Everything within the field relates to everything else. In working with couples, this involves focusing on phenomena and viewing the relationship holistically.

Principle 2: **Contemporaneity** The present field configuration also matters, not past events in isolation. The phenomenon in the therapeutic session, the behaviours, the atmosphere, and the interaction are contextualised. The field exists in the here-and-now of the couple's therapy session, though it may include present effects of past experiences. The psychological past and future are significant only insofar as they exist in the present moment of the field.

Principle 3: **Singularity** Each field is unique. Every couple's therapy session is unique. This principle recognises that while we may identify patterns or regularities, every field configuration is singular and cannot be exactly replicated. The specific constellation of people, circumstances, timing, and environmental factors creates a distinctive field that has never existed before and will never exist again in precisely the same way.

Principle 4: **Changing Process** Fields are dynamic, not static. Nothing is fixed. The field is continually constructed. This principle captures the fluid, ever-changing nature of fields. The field configuration shifts as people move, speak, think, or even breathe. The field is a continuous process of organisation and reorganisation, not a fixed structure.

Principle 5: **Possible Relevance** Every phenomenon experienced in the field is part of the total organisation and potentially meaningful. Nothing can be dismissed as irrelevant a priori. This challenges therapists to remain open to the possibility that any aspect of the field—a glance, a sound from outside, the arrangement of furniture, a fleeting thought—might become figural and significant. This principle demands a quality of focused and openly receptive attention.

These five principles may seem abstract, but they come alive in every therapeutic encounter. The following table demonstrates how each principle manifests in Siya and Sam's story and guides our therapeutic understanding:

Table 5.2 Parlett's Five Principles in Practice

Principle	*Core Concept*	*How It Appears in Siya and Sam's Story*	*Therapeutic Implications*
Organisation	Fields are organised wholes where everything relates to everything else	Sam's absence affects Siya, Priya, even the dog Pepper. The mother-in-law's influence permeates their marriage. Siya's social standing doesn't allow things to go unchanged.	View the couple's struggles holistically, not as isolated problems
Contemporaneity	Present field configuration matters most	Siya's exhaustion carries all past disappointments into this moment. The "velvet robe" metaphor emerges in the conversation. The therapist realises that she allows Siya space to talk.	Focus on how the past lives in the present rather than archaeological digging

(*Continued*)

Table 5.2 (Continued)

Principle	*Core Concept*	*How It Appears in Siya and Sam's Story*	*Therapeutic Implications*
Singularity	Each field is unique and irreplaceable	Their specific constellation of cultural expectations, family dynamics, and individual histories creates a one-of-a-kind field.	Resist applying formulaic solutions; honour each couple's uniqueness
Changing Process	Fields are dynamic, constantly reorganising	As Siya sets boundaries (moving to guest room), the entire field shifts—Sam appears in therapy, their daughter becomes protective of Siya, Siya needs change.	Stay attuned to constant flux; each session reorganises possibilities
Possible Relevance	Everything in the field potentially matters	The late session, mention of credit card statements, even the therapist's silent space-giving and tears all carry meaning.	Remain radically open; seemingly trivial details may reveal crucial dynamics

These five principles outline field theory, illustrating how its understanding leads to a radical reconceptualisation of therapeutic practice. We are invited to move beyond linear causality and isolated interventions toward a more holistic, responsive way of being with couples. Organisation reminds us that a couple's struggles cannot be understood in isolation from their total life context. Contemporaneity grounds us in the living moment, rather than relying on archaeological excavations of the past. Singularity honours the irreducible uniqueness of each couple's situation, resisting the temptation to apply formulaic solutions. Changing process keeps us attuned to the constant flux of relational life, where each breath potentially reorganises the field. And possible relevance cultivates a quality of radical openness, where even seemingly trivial moments—a phone buzzing, a shift in posture, the therapist's wandering attention—may reveal crucial dimensions of the couple's world.

As with all the stories in this book, I have written the story of Siya and Sam to illustrate how the field announces itself reflexively at first contact with the client. The felt sense of presence and absence, the weight of expectation, the invisible threads that bind and constrain—all become palpable in the therapeutic space. Like all relationships, Siya and Sam's exists within a complex field imbued with generations of cultural meaning, family mythology, and societal forces shaping love, marriage, and commitment.

Conclusion: Sensing, Participating, Transforming

Siya and Sam's story highlights how field forces appear in the therapy room as tangible, sensory experiences. The heavy velvet robe, the empty chair symbolizing

Sam's absence, and the therapist's visceral reaction are all aesthetics that depict the field.

Every therapeutic encounter—regardless of modality—involves the meeting and overlapping of individuals' fields. When therapist and client sit together, their individual fields don't merely coexist; they interpenetrate, creating something new that belongs to neither yet shapes both. This phenomenon exists whether we acknowledge it or not. This mutual influence serves as the fundamental medium where change is stimulated. By understanding the field's characteristics through Parlett's principles, we enhance our ability to move intentionally within it. We learn to identify its unique qualities, feel its textures, and perceive its dynamics. Engaging consciously in this way transforms our awareness and the nature of the field itself.

The field's capacity for self-organisation becomes visible in moments of field-emergent insight. In this instance of shared recognition, when Siya reflects, "Sometimes I think I, too, am wrapped in a velvet robe," this awareness emerges in the field.

Attuning to the field's intelligence, therapists create conditions for organic transformation. Siya's subsequent actions—setting boundaries, moving to the guest room, protecting her daughter—represent the field reorganising itself through new awareness.

As Siya walks into the city's glow at the session's end, the field continues its reorganisation. She carries the imprint of the therapeutic encounter into her life space, opening opportunities for awareness and change, resetting boundaries and gaining courage to make conscious choices for herself and her daughter.

Field theory invites us to fundamentally reimagine couples therapy—from a practice of observation and intervention to one of participation and co-creation.

What began as abstract theory—Lewin's "totality of coexisting facts"—has revealed itself as immediate, palpable experience. The heaviness in the room when Siya speaks of her isolation, the therapist's visceral response ("Oh! I'd be outta here!"), the empty chair that breathes with Sam's absence—these interesting phenomena are effects of the field, the medium through which transformation occurs.

As we prepare to explore shame in Chapter 6, we can already sense how it operates as a field force, more than an individual emotion. The velvet robe that constrains both Siya and Sam is woven from threads of cultural shame about female independence, male inadequacy, and the failure to meet traditional expectations. What we've learned about field dynamics will deepen our understanding of how shame organises entire relational fields, creating patterns that persist across generations. The phenomenological awareness we cultivated in earlier chapters has evolved into field sensitivity—a more complex form of attention that encompasses not just what appears but the invisible forces shaping appearance. This progression prepares us for the nuanced work of recognising and transforming shame as it lives in the spaces between people.

References

Francesetti, G. (2015). From individual symptoms to psychopathological fields: Towards a field perspective on clinical human suffering. *British Gestalt Journal*, 24(1), 5–19.

Francesetti, G. (2019). A clinical exploration of atmospheres: Towards a field based clinical practice. In G. Francesetti & T. Griffero (Eds.), *Psychopathology and atmospheres: Neither inside nor outside* (pp. 35–68). Cambridge Scholars Publishing.

Freud, S. (1917). *Introductory lectures on psycho-analysis (Part III)*. In J. Strachey (Ed. & Trans.), *The standard edition of the complete psychological works of Sigmund Freud* (Vol. 16, pp. 243–463). Hogarth Press.

Goldstein, K. (1939/1995). *The organism: A holistic approach to biology derived from pathological data in man*. Zone Books.

Lewin, K. (1951). *Field theory in social science: Selected theoretical papers* (D. Cartwright, Ed.). Harper & Brothers.

Parlett, M. (1991). Reflections on field theory. *The British Gestalt Journal*, 1(1), 69–80.

Perls, F., Hefferline, R., & Goodman, P. (1951/1994). *Gestalt therapy: Excitement and growth in the human personality*. The Gestalt Journal Press.

Philippson, P. (2009). *The emergent self: An existential-Gestalt approach*. Karnac Books.

Staemmler, F. (2006). A Babylonian confusion? On the uses and meanings of the term "field." *British Gestalt Journal*, 15(2), 64–83.

6 Shame, the Pathos of the Field

> "I feel like I'm disappearing. Like I'm being asked to make myself smaller and smaller."
>
> —Claudia

The Nature of Shame

Shame marks us as fundamentally relational beings. Unlike guilt, which concerns what we've done, shame strikes at who we are—our very belonging in the human community. This full-body experience of perceiving ourselves as objects under the evaluative gaze of others creates suffering so profound that most of us automatically disconnect from it (Tangney & Dearing, 2002).

From our earliest moments, shame shapes our sense of being in the world. When a toddler reaches toward danger and the parent shouts in fear, we witness shame's essential sequence: the child's startle, the flush spreading across its little features, then tears of profound distress. This isn't simply an emotion—it's the visceral discovery that we exist in relationship, that our actions reverberate through the bonds that hold us. The attuned parent repairs this rupture through embrace, transforming raw shame into a crucial teacher. Through this cycle of rupture and repair, shame becomes woven into our capacity for connection, teaching us boundaries that preserve both life and relationship.

Yet because shame hurts so acutely, we develop elaborate defences against feeling it. Fear of shame paralyses us; dissociation from shame drives addictions and perpetual conflict. We do almost anything to avoid the unbearable feeling that we don't belong. This is shame's paradox: the very emotion that confirms our need for others becomes what drives us into isolation.

Shame is the Suffering of the Field

In Chapter 5, we explored how field theory transforms our understanding of couples therapy, revealing how everything exists in mutual interdependence, how the therapeutic situation encompasses far more than individual minds meeting. We learned from Parlett (1991), how the field is organised as a whole (Organisation), exists in the present moment (Contemporaneity), is unique

DOI: 10.4324/9781003631545-10

(Singularity), constantly evolves (Changing Process), and that every phenomenon of the field matters (Possible Relevance). The therapeutic field is not a mere reflection of the couple's life. It is a living and reorganising force in the couple's relationship. The shifts in the therapy room have a ripple effect on the couple's larger field of family, culture, and community. Building on this understanding of the field, we now turn to one of its most potent and elusive emergent phenomena in therapy: shame.

To work with shame therapeutically, it helps first to understand its nature. Shame is what makes us human. It exists only in human relationships. It marks us as beings wired for connection, not isolation. Shame is the particular suffering, the pathos, that arises when a relationship is broken or potentially compromised. It serves an essential developmental function: when a protective parent chides a child approaching danger, the child's shame teaches boundaries that preserve life. The capacity to feel and acknowledge shame indicates relational health. Yet because shame hurts so acutely, we automatically suppress it. Fear of shame freezes us from taking risks; dissociation from shame drives addictions, narcissism, and perpetual conflict. We do anything to avoid feeling that we don't belong.

Writers like Lee & Wheeler (1996), Lewis (1992), Kaufman (1989) and Nathanson (1992), have provided crucial frameworks for understanding shame as a self-conscious emotion arising in interpersonal contexts. While Lewis locates shame in cognitive appraisals, and Kaufman in internalised affective schemas, the field approach insists: shame is not merely "in" the person. It is ambient, felt between bodies, sedimented into posture and silence. The therapist's task is not to "treat" it, but to become aware of how it shapes the air we breathe together. Gestalt therapy's field theory offers a radical departure from the perspective of pathology belonging exclusively to the individual. Beyond treating shame as something a person carries, we understand it as an emergent property of the entire relational field. It's not just that someone feels shame; the field itself becomes shame-laden, impacting everyone within.

This reframing fundamentally shifts our clinical approach. Instead of asking, "What's wrong with this person's shame regulation?" we inquire, "What are we sensing in this shared atmosphere? What is the quality of the emergent shame?" Field theory introduces this kind of aesthetic dimension, where we attend to the "vibe" of the room, the heaviness, the silence, the way bodies curl inward. Shame announces itself through tone, gesture, breath, and spatial dynamics long before it finds words. Most crucially, the therapist is part of the experience of the emergent pathos, feeling its weight, participating in its choreography, potentially even contributing to its presence. This process reflects Gestalt therapy's paradoxical theory of change (addressed in Chapter 3), the transformation process involves fully participating in the field (Francesetti, 2015).

The story of Liza and Claudia is creative non-fiction, aspects of which many of us find too familiar. That's only because we are not alone in the experience of shame. As we are taken through one therapy session in which this process unfolds, we witness how the field gradually reveals its hidden shame—cultural expectations about family loyalty, intergenerational patterns of female submission, and the modern-day collision between cultural values. We see how the therapist attunes to field phenomena, noticing atmospheric shifts, tracking somatic responses, allowing personal memories to inform rather than distract.

Most importantly, we observe how the connection between the partners transforms when the emotions are held. What begins as Liza's private agony—hiding her relationship, betraying either family or partner—becomes shared human experience. Through this sharing, new possibilities emerge. Not solutions or techniques, but the wisdom that arises when suffering is fully acknowledged.

Liza and Claudia: Shame and Loyalty

Liza sits on the edge of the leather armchair, her almost too lean frame coiled around her gym bag on her lap. "We're stuck in these arguments," she says with a raspy voice.

Their love story began at a rave event in Thailand, where the strobing lights and pulsing music created that magical bubble where anything feels possible. Claudia was backpacking through Southeast Asia with a friend when Liza locked eyes through the crowd. They are opposite poles of a magnet—Liza with her adventurous spirit and driven determination, Claudia with her thoughtful nature and passion for helping children find their voices through her work as a speech therapist.

Claudia sits, spine straight against the back of the sofa, pink-blonde bangs falling as she leans her head forward. "I have a lot of anxiety regarding this relationship," she states, then bites her lower lip.

"I feel like I am being disrespected," she elaborates.

"Disrespected, how so?" I ask.

"My identity is being compromised in this relationship," Claudia continues, her accent thickening slightly. "Whenever I come to Singapore, I am asked to hide who we are together. To pretend we're just friends. To erase myself."

Watching her partner speak, Liza smiles. She looks almost sad, her eyes tender. "That is true," she acknowledges, barely above a whisper. "It is because my family cannot know about us."

The silence that follows is a weighty muck surrounding us. Her gentle smile fades to flatness as she looks down at her hands, clasped tightly in her lap.

Claudia's eyes darken, and she looks suddenly livid. "I heard what happened over the festivities," she says. "Please don't get me wrong. I understand why you're afraid. But Liza..."

"My dad actually said it," says Liza. She recalls the festive lunch where her father, surrounded by extended family, declared she was no longer his daughter. All because, at thirty-three, with dual postgraduate degrees and a successful career, she had "dared" to move out.

Claudia reaches out, then pulls her hand back. "Your cousin who supported you," she says, "she still talks to you, right? There are people in your family who do understand…"

"One person," Liza corrects her. "One cousin who could only manage a silent nod while everyone else turned on me. While another cousin's husband demanded I ask for forgiveness for being 'brainwashed by social media influence.'" Liza turns to me and continues, "He even chided my father for educating his daughters, saying, 'This is what you get in return.' He even swore never to allow his girls to get that far."

Claudia wasn't there at the scene, but she had heard Liza recount this moment enough times.

I hear the stories of cultural rivalries and the complexities of family pride and shame; still, they leave me in disbelief whenever I encounter them. Liza's story surprises me as it is unique in post-pandemic Singapore, especially having such an impact on someone with Liza's profile.

Liza adds, "My parents wouldn't even look at me."

Liza and I exchange a glance; an electric stillness surrounds us. The burden of unspoken words weighs heavily between us. The hum of the air conditioner drowns out the pounding in my chest, emotions mirroring the look in Claudia's eyes.

"I find no words to adequately express how impacted I am by what you have just shared," I say.

Claudia gazes forward, her big eyes unfocused and distant; the harsh truth of our situation hits her. If her father finds Liza being a woman of our times unacceptable, then what about her being in a same-sex relationship? "So we keep hiding," she says. "When I visit Singapore, I become your 'friend from Amsterdam.' We carefully calculate how long we can look at each other in public."

"We…" Her voice catches slightly. "We pretend."

The weight of enforced self-concealment is a burlap shroud that smothers us.

"I don't ask this lightly," Liza whispers. "Every time I introduce you as my friend and every moment we must keep our distance in public, it hurts."

Claudia presses her fingers to her temples, struggling to articulate something that feels almost forbidden to say. "I'm disappearing. Like I'm being asked to make myself smaller and smaller."

"I don't understand," she continues. "How can you want to maintain connections with people who treat you this way? Who would humiliate their own in front of others? Who…"

She stops abruptly. "And then I feel terrible for even thinking this."

"What is terrible about what you are thinking?" I ask.

"I'm supposed to be better than this, am I not? I'm supposed to uphold inclusion and diversity." Claudia's voice drops to almost a whisper. She recollects carefree childhood days in a scenic countryside village in Tirol. She also remembers being told in school, "We don't use the word 'race.'"

"Yet here I am, feeling this…this rage against your family's control, against their beliefs." The torment in her voice is palpable with the increase in register. She then slumps onto the backrest of the sofa with a thud.

"Somehow, it's not easy to get things right, is it?" I reflect.

"No," Claudia whispers, "it's not." She looks at Liza, who has been silently weeping. "I feel like a fraud. Here I am feeling this revulsion. And then I really, really hate myself for feeling it."

At the sound of the word "hate," I notice us instinctively jabbing our fingernails into our forearms. I draw this synchronicity to their attention and suggest we reflect on what we're doing for a moment.

"Let's tune in to what comes up for us," I say.

The silence blares. Then, a warmth of comfort sets in. Solidarity.

"Pain," Liza says, reaching across the space between them, her hand resting gently on Claudia's knee as if to soothe her while needing to soothe herself. "I'm protecting my mother's pain," she says, her voice heavy. "I'm carrying it because it is also mine."

The room is silent. Within this quiet, there is a pervasive feminine energy—Claudia's internal conflict between European ideals and deep emotions, Liza bearing a legacy of family expectations, and I, part of the moment. Amidst all this, I am also conscious of another important woman: Liza's mother, an unseen yet present figure. "I wonder, Liza, what it would be like if your mother were to be in this room," I say.

Liza straightens her posture and speaks about her mother, a gentle woman who cooks unforgettable spicy dishes and was a straight-A student during her O-level years. A woman of her time, she was convinced that it was better to marry her childhood friend and neighbour than pursue higher education. She believed it would be sufficient for her spouse to provide for her, and he did. Liza's father is a devoted husband. Nonetheless, the mom ensured that her daughter received all the educational opportunities she could attain.

As Liza recalls that family gathering, she brings up the image of her mother sitting silently, grappling with the turmoil around her, her husband talking about disowning her daughter while relatives hurl accusations.

"I feel responsible for her pain. For bringing this disgrace upon her," Liza continues.

Claudia and I nod, acknowledging the heaviness of the situation.

I momentarily transport myself to my grandmother's kitchen, where the rich aroma of home-cooked stew fills the air. In that moment, I feel the warm familiarity of an extended family gathering—where clear gender roles exist, with fathers and mothers each knowing their place in an age-old dance. There is the comfort of authentic traditional spices, the security of togetherness, and the safety of protection that extends beyond the individual to encompass the whole clan. This is what Liza's family offers—something many Western families have traded away in pursuit of individual freedom. The loyalty that forms their very identity, the belonging that doesn't need to be earned or proved. Yet with this profound gift comes profound vulnerability: the fear that what they have cherished and protected across generations could be taken away, their carefully preserved identity dissolved by forces no one can control.

I blink, grounding myself again with my clients. Like traditional cooking, therapeutic change is a slow, sometimes uncomfortable process—a breaking down and reconstitution, layer by layer. Claudia and Liza begin the process of finding their way. Over time, their relationship will simmer, and their differences will blend and transform into something uniquely theirs.

Shame in the Background and Foreground

The story of Liza and Claudia reveals how shame saturates the therapeutic field without ever being explicitly named. Like humidity in the air, it pervades every gesture, every silence, every painful revelation. The evidence accumulates through phenomenological details: Liza's "almost too lean frame coiled around her gym bag"—a body made small, protective. Her voice dropped to "barely above a whisper" when acknowledging the truth. The "weighty muck" of silence that follows her admission. Claudia's rigid spine against the sofa, her fingers pressed to her temples, the struggle to articulate what feels "almost forbidden to say."

Shame manifests somatically. When Claudia speaks of feeling like "a fraud" and hating herself for her feelings, all three women—clients and therapist—unconsciously jab their fingernails into their forearms. Shame doesn't exist exclusively in one person but emerges between bodies, creating a shared choreography of pain.

The therapist's sensitivity to these field phenomena allows the gradual sharpening of shame from background to foreground. She notices atmospheric shifts. She tracks her own somatic responses: the pounding in her chest, her jaw clenching at the image of Liza kneeling. Rather than interpreting or intervening, she stays present with these sensations, allowing them to inform the therapeutic process.

In this story, we witness shame's many layers:

- **Intergenerational shame**: Liza carries her mother's pain—the shame of the educated woman who chose marriage over career, now watching her daughter suffer for making different choices, and being helpless at defending her daughter.
- **Cultural shame turned to humiliation**: Liza's family, unable to endure the pain of shame caused by their daughter's rejection of their traditional identity due to modern foreign influences, outwardly expresses it through public humiliation. The cousin's husband, who "chided my father for educating his daughters," shows how shame about cultural change is disowned and used as a weapon.
- **The shame of being compelled to conceal identity**: Every time Claudia is introduced as "just a friend," and every calculated glance in public, it deepens

the shame of denying one's identity and succumbing to prejudice. "We pretend," Claudia says, the burden of concealment pressing down on them like "a burlap shroud."

- **Shame about shame**: Claudia's meta-shame emerges powerfully—shame about feeling rage toward Liza's family, shame about not living up to her progressive ideals. "I'm supposed to be better than this," she whispers, her upbringing with its colour-blind idealism colliding with visceral revulsion.

The therapeutic breakthrough occurs when shame transforms from individual burden to shared experience. "Let's tune in to what comes up for us."

In that shared silence with the pathos, something shifts. The "warmth of comfort" and "sense of solidarity" that follows marks shame's transformation from isolating force to connective tissue. When acknowledged together rather than endured alone, shame reveals its deeper truth: we are bound by our vulnerability, our need for belonging, our terror of rejection. Shame is suffered in the breakdown of a relationship, and it is healed through contact.

Conclusion

Throughout this chapter, we have explored shame as the pathos of the field—not merely an individual emotion but a phenomenon that emerges between people, saturating the therapeutic atmosphere and shaping every interaction. Shame marks us as fundamentally relational beings: we feel shame only because we need others, yet this very need makes us vulnerable to rejection and judgment. As we witnessed with Liza and Claudia, shame manifests through multiple layers—cultural expectations, family loyalty, sexual identity, and the meta-shame of feeling ashamed about our responses.

Their story illuminates a crucial paradox: there is no relationship without the threat of shame. To connect with another is to risk being seen, judged, and potentially rejected. Yet it is not shame itself that creates our deepest suffering, but rather our fear of shame—the elaborate defences we construct to avoid this fundamental human experience. These defences drive the maladaptive behaviours we see throughout couples therapy: Liza's compliance with family humiliation, Claudia's self-hatred for her authentic responses, the endless hiding and pretending that erodes their connection.

In Chinese, shame translates to "沒面子" (méi miànzi)—literally "no face"—capturing how shame fundamentally concerns being seen and recognised by others. Face represents one's social capital, carefully accumulated through proper behaviour and easily lost through transgression (Hwang, 1987; Ho, 1976). This linguistic insight reveals what Western psychology often misses: shame is never just internal but always exists in the field of relationships.

In Malay, "malu" encompasses both shame and shyness, functioning as a social regulator that maintains harmony (Goddard, 1996). It can be both negative (shame from wrongdoing) and positive (appropriate modesty). This dual nature illuminates shame's potential as a teacher—what Heider (1990) calls "the guardian of social norms." The very existence of positive malu suggests that shame, when properly understood, guides ethical living rather than crushing the spirit.

Whether expressed as "no face" or as social harmony, these terms remind us that shame always exists in the space between people.

These linguistic gifts deepen our phenomenological understanding. Rather than imposing Western categories, we let each language teach us about shame's multiple dimensions. These cultural perspectives point toward shame's transformative potential. When we stop defending against shame and instead develop a response-ability—the capacity to respond rather than react—shame becomes a teacher rather than a tormentor. This requires a delicate balance: to touch and experience shame fully, then let it move through us rather than fleeing the experience.

As we turn to Chapter 7, we will explore the adaptation of Gestalt therapy's contact cycle in couples therapy—how couples move between connection and withdrawal in natural rhythms. We'll see how the fear of shame interrupts this flow, freezing partners in fixed positions, unable to move freely between closeness and distance. Chapter 8 will then introduce creative indifference, a philosophy of radical acceptance that offers an antidote to shame's painful effects. This centred stance allows us to hold differences without judgement, creating space where partners can be fully themselves without shame or shaming.

References

Francesetti, G. (2015). From individual symptoms to psychopathological fields: Towards a field perspective on clinical human suffering. *British Gestalt Journal*, 24(1), 5–19.

Goddard, C. (1996). The "social emotions" of Malay (Bahasa Melayu). *Ethos*, 24(3), 426–464.

Heider, K. G. (1990). *Landscapes of emotion: Mapping three cultures of emotion in Indonesia*. Cambridge University Press.

Ho, D. Y. F. (1976). On the concept of face. *American Journal of Sociology*, 81(4), 867–884.

Hwang, K. K. (1987). Face and favor: The Chinese power game. *American Journal of Sociology*, 92(4), 944–974.

Kaufman, G. (1989). *The psychology of shame: Theory and treatment of shame-based syndromes*. Springer.

Lee, R. G. & Wheeler, G. (Eds.). (1996). *The voice of shame: Silence and connection in psychotherapy*. Jossey-Bass.

Lewis, M. (1992). *Shame: The exposed self*. Free Press.

Nathanson, D. L. (1992). *Shame and pride: Affect, sex, and the birth of the self*. W. W. Norton & Company.

Parlett, M. (1991). Reflections on field theory. *British Gestalt Journal*, 1(2), 69–81.

Tangney, J. P. & Dearing, R. L. (2002). *Shame and guilt*. Guilford Press.

7 The Cycle of Connection

Movement Between Contact and Withdrawal

> "I ha[ve craved all my life to be seen, and yet being seen is so difficult, so utterly painful."
>
> David (from Chapter 4)

Beyond Fusion: The Connection Model

The fusion concept of marriage, deeply embedded in society for over 4,000 years, influences our expectations of marriage today. Like fish unaware of water, we move through this fusion model without recognising its effects on individuals or considering whether it can be achieved without affecting the institution of marriage. As Resnick observes, "If you're a microbe on a stop sign, you'd think the whole world is red."

The fusion model emerged in historical contexts where human survival depended on belonging to tightly knit communities. In societies with short life expectancies, limited medical knowledge, and rigid social structures, the merging of two into one served essential functions. It ensured economic stability, clear roles, and community cohesion. The model worked for its time—when marriages lasted perhaps twenty years before death intervened, when patriarchal structures went unquestioned, when individual fulfilment ranked far below collective survival.

In contemporary Western contexts, partners now seek emotional fulfilment, personal growth, and a depth of emotional connection (Perel, 2006; Gottman & Gottman, 2015). Meanwhile, many other cultures still find meaning and stability in relationship models that prioritise family harmony, clear roles, and community integration. Traditional gender roles that were accepted in past generations are becoming less clear-cut in some societies, while remaining valued in others.

Statistics on rising divorce rates and declining marriages worldwide tell part of the story. Resnick points us towards a more worrying reality: among those who remain married, a significant number are effectively "secretly miserably married." People may stay in such relationships for their children's sake, financial security, fear of loneliness, or religious reasons—rarely because the relationship genuinely sustains them. Phrases like "yes, dear" and "whatever you

DOI: 10.4324/9781003631545-11

want, honey" conceal disconnection. Depression, addiction, and quiet desperation often fill the void where connection should be. Our negative view of marriage might ultimately lead to a life of solitude, regardless.

Neither model is inherently superior—each meets different social and individual needs. Many cultures successfully maintain fusion-based relationships that provide security, meaning, and belonging. The connection model offers an alternative for couples seeking to balance individual autonomy with intimate partnership, giving priority to two separate individuals who choose to dance together while staying true to themselves. This model acknowledges authentic difference as essential for awareness and connection. We can't feel the water that matches our exact body temperature when we're immersed in it—we need a difference to know where we end, and the world begins. The same principle applies to relationships: without difference, there can be little sense of the self and the other.

As we explored in Chapter 6, shame emerges precisely at this contact boundary—that vital edge where differences meet. Contact is the connective tissue of relationships, yet paradoxically, it's also where shame resides most intensely. When we approach the boundary where authentic meeting becomes possible, we inevitably encounter the pathos of shame—that fundamental human emotion that both confirms our need for connection and threatens to drive us into isolation. This is why intimacy feels so treacherous: it requires us to transcend shame in the most extreme way, demanding a total abandonment of self-scrutiny at the very moment when we feel most exposed.

Understanding the Cycle of Connection

Healthy relationships move through natural rhythms, like breathing or the tides. The Resnicks identified five phases that couples continuously navigate, each serving essential functions in maintaining both connection and individual integrity. Building on the Resnicks' five phases, the following wave diagram illustrates the fluid movement between withdrawal, contact, intimacy, confluence, and isolation.

1. **Withdrawal** represents the necessary retreat for restoration and self-nourishment. Like sleep restores the body, withdrawal restores the self. Partners turn inward, engage in solitary activities, and process their experiences. This isn't abandonment or rejection—it's the inhale that makes the next exhale possible.
2. **Contact** occurs at the boundary where differences meet. Here, one person's lived experience touches another's, creating the spark of recognition: "You are you, and I am me, and here we meet." Contact requires courage to be authentic with one's emotions and be ready to perceive the other as genuinely distinct. To support this condition, partners intentionally accept and are curious about their differences, expressing their thoughts and lived experiences.

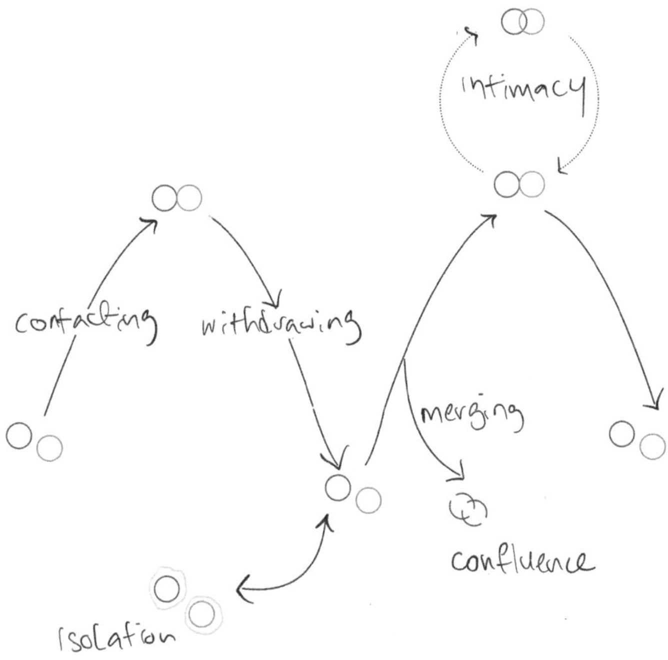

Figure 7.1 A Wave Representation of the Resnick Model of Coupling.

3 **Intimacy** deepens contact into a surrender of oneself in the presence of the other. In this phase, scrutinising oneself, self-judgement and putting on an impression are suspended. There is a feeling of safety in this openness, with no need to self-monitor. They are simply together.
4 **Confluence** allows for temporary merging. Individual boundaries become obscured. Confluent experiences are peaceful, compromising and harmonious. It is the "I want what you want" moment. Unlike the fusion model's permanent confluence, healthy confluence is intentional and naturally transitory.
5 **Isolation** provides a protective space when the individual feels overwhelmed by being in the system. Here is where boundaries are coated with a barrier. Sometimes we need space from each other to rest and defragment. After conflict, disappointment, or when flooded with emotion, isolation allows time to regroup, consider, reflect and self-regulate before attempting contact again. A chronic tendency to stay in isolation can happen and would be disruptive to the relationship.

Each phase plays a crucial role in healthy relationships, as couples ideally flow between these different states. Problems arise when couples become stuck in any single phase, unable to move naturally through the cycle. These interruptions to the flow typically occur unconsciously, often driven by underlying guilt or shame. When couples become frozen in one position—whether perpetually withdrawn, excessively merged, or defensively isolated—the relationship loses its vitality.

Contact vs. Connection: A Crucial Distinction

Understanding the difference between contact and connection highlights why many couples feel both close and distant. Contact refers to specific moments of encounter at the edge of difference. For example, when John's tears fell as he heard Sarah's story of abandonment, when Liam whispered "I get you" to his absent father, or when Emma and James's hands finally met on the exercise ball—these were moments where the individual moved towards contact with themselves and with the present others.

Connection embodies the whole dance—the rhythm of approaching and withdrawing, touching and parting, merging and differentiating. A connected couple can move smoothly through all stages of the cycle. They have developed a relational musicality—knowing when to draw close, when to step back, when to lead, and when to follow.

The distinction between contact and connection illuminates why our therapeutic work focuses on restoring movement rather than forcing proximity. When couples lose their ability to flow through the cycle, they often present in therapy frozen in defensive positions—some perpetually merged, others rigidly separate. The therapist's involvement in the field supports this movement. The couples from our previous chapters each demonstrate unique patterns of stuckness and the varied pathways back to fluid movement.

How Our Couples Got Stuck and What Therapy Did

So far, we've witnessed eight couples in this book, each demonstrating unique patterns of interruption in their connection. Rather than abstract categories, let's examine how these real therapeutic encounters revealed specific ways couples become frozen in defensive positions, and more importantly, how the therapeutic process facilitated movement.

1 *Sarah and John: Frozen in Isolation*

How They Got Stuck: Sarah and John had retreated so completely from each other that they'd lost even the memory of being untethered while together. Their careful positioning spoke of two people who'd given up on the possibility of connecting. Unlike healthy isolation that provides temporary respite, theirs had calcified into permanent distance.

What Therapy Did: The therapist invited John to experiment with being "easy-going," to stop his anxious pursuit. This created even more space initially, paradoxically sharpening Sarah's awareness of what she'd been missing. When she said, "I miss the John I once knew," the first tentative reach toward contact emerged. The shared memory of forbidden music—their teenage rebellion—became the bridge across decades of isolation.

2 *Liam and Akina: Conflicting Withdrawal Patterns*

How They Got Stuck: Both partners needed withdrawal, but in incompatible ways that are almost dissociative. Liam's drinking represented an escape from overwhelm, while Akina's sleep was both self-protection and the only rebellion available to her. Their withdrawals triggered each other's deepest fears—his terror of abandonment meeting her history of enforced wakefulness—creating a spiral where each partner's protective strategy increased the other's distress.

What Therapy Did: Through phenomenological exploration, the therapist helped them become aware of their childhood adaptations that shaped current patterns. When Liam could finally see his father's struggle in his own ("Pa, I get it. I get you. I get me"), the compulsive quality of his withdrawal softened. Compassion replaced reactivity, allowing for conscious choice about when and how to withdraw.

3 Emma and James: Parallel Lives in Rigid Withdrawal

How They Got Stuck: They'd constructed elaborate separate worlds isolated from each other—his nightly dinners at his mother's, her scheduled absences. Their children became the only conduit for communication, a pattern that reinforced their disconnection.

What Therapy Did: The simple act of rolling an exercise ball between them bypassed their verbal defences. This wordless physical exchange created the first genuine contact in years. The ball's back-and-forth movement embodied the rhythm of connection they'd lost, teaching their bodies what their hearts had forgotten.

4 Mei and Markus: Forced Confluence vs. Protective Isolation

How They Got Stuck: Markus demanded confluence—expecting Mei to merge with his vision of family, to be a symbolic substitute mother to his children. Her defending of her boundaries appeared to him as withdrawal and non-communication, triggering his criticism. Neither could see the other's position: his grief over separation from his children, her self-protection from a lifetime of being oppressed.

What Therapy Did: Instead of mediating their positions, the therapist supported each in fully expressing their inner truth. When the therapist acknowledged the reality—"They remain a 12-hour flight away"—Markus could finally feel his grief rather than displacing it onto Mei. Her declaration, "I am not their mother," wasn't rejection but healthy boundary-setting that created space for openness.

5 Sherlyn and Derrick: Barriers to Moving from Contact to Intimacy

How They Got Stuck: They wanted to be intimate but invisible audiences crowded their life space. The internalised voices of family and church created a shame barrier, interrupting their contact and intimacy. They remained frozen at the threshold, unspontaneous and unable to move forward.

What Therapy Did: Making the invisible visible through empty chair work allowed them to address these judging phantom eyes directly. When Sherlyn could tell the "watchers" to leave and Derrick could "speak to his father" in an empty chair, they learned to feel into their experiences and allowed themselves to express feelings that were retroflected.

6 Hai and David: Cycling Between Extremes

How They Got Stuck: They oscillated in a stratosphere of deflection. Neither could find ground for authentic meeting. Their matching footwear suggested a yearning for connection, but their interaction pattern kept them feeling disconnected from each other.

What Therapy Did: The role reversal experiment took their conversations beyond the superficial, with each partner embodying the other's posture. When David felt Hai's exhausted vigilance and Hai experienced David's lostness, and when both saw their reflections in the other's posturing, empathy replaced discontent.

7 Siya and Sam: Confluence Without Contact

How They Got Stuck: Siya's increasing need to detach herself from the pull towards the confluence that defined her marriage led her to seek therapy. Shame and guilt at the boundary of difference made it difficult for Siya to recognise her needs and to step out of the role imposed upon her.

What Therapy Did: Therapy provided Siya with an environment where she could hear herself—a position she had never experienced before. By giving space to her voice, she was able to make choices that were protective of herself and her child.

8 Liza and Claudia: Cultural Shame Interrupting Flow

How They Got Stuck: The necessity to hide their same-sex relationship from family strained their relationship. Shame organised their field, with both partners grappling with their ideological and cultural introjects, leaving their relationship laden with pain and conflict.

What Therapy Did: Sharing the embodied pathos of shame during the session, something shifted. There was no rush to address cultural realities (which would have been an endless task). Being together in contact with suffering transformed the relationship from one of pain to one of healing.

The following table summarises how each couple's unique interruption in the connection cycle manifested and how therapy facilitated movement:

Every couple has a natural emotional rhythm that ebbs and flows between them, and the connection cycle helps them rediscover this unique rhythm. By finding their own path back to movement, whether through dramatic breakthroughs or subtle changes, they can bring new life to their relationships.

Table 7.1 Couples' Interruptions in the Connection Cycle

Couple	*Stuck Phase*	*Pattern of Interruption*	*What Prevented Movement*	*How Therapy Facilitated Flow*
Sarah & John	Frozen in isolation	Complete retreat, lost memory of connection	Decades of careful distance; giving up on possibility	Experiment with "being easy-going" created space for awareness; shared music memory bridged isolation
Liam & Akina	Conflicting withdrawal	Both withdraw but trigger each other's fears	His drinking = escape; her sleep = protection; incompatible patterns	Recognising childhood adaptations; compassion replaced reactivity
Emma & James	Rigid withdrawal to isolation from the other/ parallel lives	Elaborate separate worlds, children as only conduit	His mother's house; her scheduled absences	Therapist's involvement; a wordless ball exchange taught bodies the rhythm they'd forgotten
Mei & Markus	Forced confluence vs. isolation	He demands merging; she protects boundaries	His grief displaced onto her; her lifetime of oppression	Supporting full expression of truth; acknowledging "12-hour flight away" reality
Sherlyn & Derrick	Barrier of shame between contact & intimacy	Frozen at threshold, unable to deepen	Invisible audiences (family/ church) creating shame barrier	Empty chair work to address phantom presences directly
Hai & David	Cycling between isolation and confluence, no contact	Superficiality and yearning	Excessive managing vs. paralysis; no middle ground	Embodied role experiment to embody other's position; empathy and vulnerability expressed
Siya & Sam	Confluence without contact	He's confluent with mother; expects traditional wife role	Shame/guilt at boundaries; cultural field forces	Supporting Siya's boundaries; witnessing Sam's struggle to individuate
Liza & Claudia	Pull to confluence, unaware of shame in the field	Avoiding shame by being defensive and/or self-hating	Need to hide one's identity; ideological introjects	Sharing embodied shame experience; witnessing without fixing

Conclusion

Throughout this chapter, we have examined the Resnicks' connection cycle, which highlights the natural rhythm of relationships. This cycle is a continuous flow between withdrawal, contact, intimacy, confluence, and isolation. Each couple's story in this book shows how they experience unique interruptions to this flow, illustrating that relational distress often stems not from too much difference, but from an inability to move smoothly through the cycle together.

Some of the most profound disruptions occur when partners are at different stages in the cycle—one reaching out for connection while the other pulls away, one seeking intimacy while the other withdraws. Such misalignment gives rise to painful feelings of separation, loneliness, rejection, and disappointment—like dancers dancing to different tunes. Unless we move towards contact, true intimacy (distinguished from sexual prowess) also becomes unattainable. Trying to address sexual difficulties without first establishing a connection is like building on shaky ground, a recipe for resentment and conflict.

Our work isn't about teaching couples the "right" way to navigate the cycle. Instead, we're guided by Beisser's paradoxical theory of change (1970), which encourages us to help couples fully experience their disruptions—what partners do to avoid being present, how they truly are, and what gets in the way of them seeing themselves and each other.

Contact, as Resnick and Resnick remind us, is the connective tissue of relationships, yet it's precisely at the boundary where two individuals meet that shame resides. This is why contact feels both life-giving and treacherous. As we explored in Chapter 6, shame exists at the very edge of contact between individuals—that vulnerable moment when we risk being truly seen by another. This makes us want to withdraw and self-isolate. Our work in relationships requires transcending shame, not avoiding its experience.

The connection model offers hope because it normalises this struggle: of moving towards and withdrawing, of being like you and asserting my uniqueness. Unlike the fusion model that seeks a consistent shame-free merger, the connection model acknowledges that we can risk feeling the pain of shame, together: to tolerate, even embrace, the vulnerability that comes with contact.

As we prepare for the next chapter, we turn to Friedlaender's creative indifference—a philosophy central to Gestalt therapy that echoes the ancient wisdom of the Taoist's yin–yang. This principle of holding the centre between polarities becomes crucial when navigating the most challenging aspects of couples' therapy: when relationships come to an end. Creative indifference provides a way to stay present with opposing forces—the urge to save a marriage versus the need to part, and the desire for reconciliation versus the reality of irrevocable rupture. Through Ben and Jenn's confrontation with betrayal and Siya and Sam's journey toward conscious uncoupling, we will explore how therapists can uphold a centred presence amidst these potent polarities. Even as the familiar dance concludes, creative indifference shows how separation can honour the dance of difference, allowing partners to part with dignity while preserving what remains sacred between them.

References

Beisser, A. (1970). The paradoxical theory of change. In J. Fagan & I. L. Shepherd (Eds.), *Gestalt therapy now* (pp. 77–80). Science and Behavior Books.

Gottman, J. M. & Gottman, J. S. (2015). *The seven principles for making marriage work.* Harmony Books.

Perel, E. (2006). *Mating in captivity: Unlocking erotic intelligence.* Harper.

Resnick, R. F. & Resnick, R. W. (2020, September 7). *From fusion to connection model of relationship [Video].* YouTube. https://www.youtube.com/watch?v=TslbJCA4yuE

Part IV

Integration and Practice

8 Creative Indifference

Conflict and the Therapist's Centred Presence

"To break down right now would be a luxury I can't afford."

—Jenn

"Sometimes the truest act of love is the courage to be real."

—Therapist

Creative Indifference: An Introduction

The therapy room holds its breath. In this session, we witness betrayal and the trail of pain it leaves behind. Between partners, a chasm stretches, impossible to bridge. Every instinct urges the therapist to jump to action—to comfort, to confront, to somehow fix this shattered terrain. The therapist remains still, holding a different kind of presence. One that is silent yet laden with the understanding that in this space lie possibilities. This is creative indifference in practice, an active capacity to hold space for all that is.

Creative indifference represents perhaps Gestalt therapy's most profound and overlooked contribution to therapeutic practice (Frambach, 2003; Perls, Hefferline & Goodman, 1951). The term itself creates confusion—how can a therapist be "indifferent" while working with couples in crisis? Yet this concept, originating from philosopher Salomo Friedlaender's *Schöpferische Indifferenz* (1918), offers something essential: a way of being present with polarities, conflicts, and differences, staying in the "fertile void" of that central position without collapsing into either side or forcing premature resolution.

Polarities are the essence of differences, and differences are integral in relationships. One partner seeks intimacy, while the other requires space. One communicates through emotion, the other through logic. Cultural values clash; past and present collide. The therapeutic instinct is to "help" clients resolve these tensions to suggest compromise, understanding, communication techniques, or behavioural agreements. Creative indifference, however, proposes a radical alternative: What if the tension itself is not the problem but the lack of awareness and acceptance of it?

DOI: 10.4324/9781003631545-13

We have seen polarities as a phenomenon with the couples throughout this book, from John's (Chapter 1) wish to be "carefree" versus his need to be a responsible father and husband, to Liam's (Chapter 2) desire for closeness against his need for space, and Emma and James's (Chapter 4) longing for the warmth of connection versus the icy rift from each other. In this chapter, we will understand how creative indifference has moved the therapeutic change along, and how the other Gestalt therapy principles support the therapist's ability to practice with creative indifference. We will explore the power of adopting Friedlaender's teachings through the stories of two couples facing major crises, testing this philosophy as Ben and Jenn confront the immediate aftermath of revealed affairs, while Siya and Sam consider the possibility of ending their marriage.

Case Study A: Ben and Jenn—the Shattered Field of Infidelity

Ben and Jenn enter my office, and I sense the chilling atmosphere of a courtroom. My usual opening question, "And what brings you here this morning?" falls flat, no bounce, no ping, just a dull thud.

I am driven to act, to do something. I am disturbed by the stillness. I stay silent. I observe the juxtaposition of their current tension against the signs of familiarity they share. Ten years of marriage have left their imprint in small ways—the unconscious mirroring of postures, the way they occupy space together despite their current rift. Their carefully maintained appearances—her crisp business suit, his pressed shirt—speak of the life they've built. In these first moments, it was evident that something beneath that polished surface had fractured.

"It's all a lie. My marriage." Jenn's voice finally breaks the silence, flat and hollow. "All of it."

He's been having affairs with other women, and it's not just recently. He has been at it since the beginning. Ten years." Each word falls like an axe. "And everyone knew. His friends. Our friends. Everyone but me."

Her voice cuts through the silence. Her dry eyes meet mine. I don't ask how she feels—her posture says enough. She adds with a sharp edge, "I have no tears left. I wept alone for four days." She had uncovered his love messages to the other women on his computer while he was on a diving trip.

Ben sits still, his gaze fixed on me with an expression of someone waiting for judgement, punishment, absolution—something. When he finally speaks, his words come out in fragments, each piece carefully measured: "I was incapacitated… It's not what you think."

"I'm not quite sure what you imagine I'm thinking now," I say.

He responds, "I just want us to be back together. Back with my family."

Jenn says nothing.

Truth surfaces in fragments. He recounts how he has maintained a long-term relationship with a divorced woman from his previous job. She has a young child. There were other women. He had adeptly juggled his double life until it came to light.

For Jenn, ten years of shared memories are eclipsed. Their two children are playing blissfully at home, unaware that their world has shifted on its axis. Between Ben and Jenn lies a deep crater of pain.

"I needed this session. My mind has been spinning nonstop for four weeks. A vortex turning and turning, always returning to the same question." Jenn presses her fingertips to her temples as if trying to still the relentless motion inside her head. "Why?"

That timeless question, I think to myself. I've discovered that "why" is a gateway leading into a boundless corridor of reflections where solutions are seldom found that truly mend.

"I've shared all I can with Jenn," he states, raising his hands in a way that appears more defensive than resigned. "I'll cease all contact with her. I'm truly, truly sorry." His words sound weak—his left cheek twitches.

I look towards the far end of the room. I allow myself to feel upset, even angry, in silence.

"My kids are still so young," Jenn says. Then, straightening her spine, she clears her throat. "To break down right now would be a luxury I can't afford. To get hysterical, to punish him, to do any of the things I want to do; it's all a luxury. My children are too young."

"Yes," I say simply, acknowledging how she finds herself alone in supporting their children's world, the only reality they understand.

I reach for my ceramic mug, taking a slow sip of water. I settle.

"Why? I just need to know why." Jenn repeats, her eyes finding mine.

"And you are looking for answers," I acknowledge.

Her response unleashes like a breaking dam, "I need to understand how he could do this to me, to us. Did he ever think about our children? Why her?" Each question is a body blow. "What made her so special that he could throw away everything we built?"

"Those would have been my questions, too, Jenn," I say.

"I couldn't help it," says Ben. "I feel lonely in our marriage. You're always—"

My throat tightens at his mention of "you." I feel a surge rise within me, "This is not your moment, Ben."

"What is it about me that makes you go to her?" Jenn asks again.

Ben says nothing. His face flushes, tears threatening.

"I'm attracted to her, well, because she actually needs me." His words land like a plane crash.

The audacity of his response is my immediate thought. I decide to set it aside. The following silence feels dense and heavy.

Jenn's hands tremble. She wraps her arms around herself as if she were freezing in the room. "So do I and our boys."

She sobs.

Ben contorts his face. "What should we do now?"

I can't answer that question. I meet his gaze, feeling the fear in his eyes. My eyes drift to a child's crayon drawing of a giraffe on the wall, its uneven lines and disproportionate features revealing more honesty than any adult effort at perfection. The drawing reminds me of what truly matters: somewhere, two children are waiting for their father to return, their world still intact in their eyes.

"Ben, there are no 'shoulds' for Jenn right now. The consequences of your actions are yours to bear. Considering your children, it is hard for me to justify prioritising your needs right now." I let the words land from a place in me shaped by my mentors. They were men who practised with clarity and kindness.

"That's what I needed to hear." Jenn's voice is barely audible through her tears.

I nod. "Yes, Jenn."

The weightiness in the room lifts.

Taking the Creative Centre

Infidelity causes a seismic upheaval that reaches far beyond just breaching trust. For the deceived partner, the revelation shatters the very foundation of their life, sparking a spiral of intense emotions and punishing ruminations. The therapeutic environment becomes charged with raw emotion—fear, humiliation, shame, and blame create a visceral atmosphere of pain that physically manifests in the room. This experience offers valuable insight into what the field needs in the moment.

The Therapist's Position: Acknowledging and Bracketing Bias

In situations like these, the therapist faces an immediate internal challenge. Reading Ben and Jenn's story, the therapist experiences visceral responses—protective anger toward Jenn, revulsion at Ben's apparent lack of remorse, and frustration with his self-centred responses. These physiological reactions—the tightening in the throat, the surge of moral outrage—are not distractions from therapeutic work but vital information about what's alive in the field.

The first step toward creative indifference involves acknowledging these biases rather than suppressing them. The therapist recognises her anger at Ben's attitude given the gravity of the situation, her impulse to comfort Jenn, her desire to see justice served. This acknowledgement is crucial—by naming these internal reactions, the therapist can begin the process of bracketing them, setting them aside without personal agenda while remaining fully engaged with the field's emotional reality.

Attuning to the Pathos in the Field

From this acknowledged position, the therapist actively attunes to the pathos—the suffering—present in the field. For Jenn, this manifests as humiliation—an intense experience of shame imposed by another's deception. Humiliation differs from ordinary shame in its relational nature; it requires the actions of another to create the experience of being diminished, exposed, and made vulnerable (Klein, 1991). This imposed shame becomes the emotional landscape Jenn must navigate while maintaining stability for her children.

For Ben, the pathos appears as fear and flight from despair. His defensive responses and attempts at quick solutions reveal a man drowning in consequences he never imagined, desperately seeking escape from the weight of his choices. His fear of losing his family is compounded by his inability to comprehend the depth of damage fully his actions have caused.

Schöpferisch: *Divine Creation, Not Artistic Imagination*

The "creative" in creative indifference—Friedlaender's original word, *Schöpferisch*, carries deep theological implications. This term implies creating as God creates, bringing something into existence from nothing, rather than ***kreativ***, which suggests artistic imagination or rearrangement of existing materials. This distinction is vital for understanding the therapist's role. At the zero point, the therapist doesn't imagine solutions or craft interventions but creates space for new possibilities to germinate from the field itself.

Indifference, in this context, means setting aside personal bias and agenda. The therapist becomes a conduit for what wants to emerge rather than an agent of predetermined outcomes. This requires profound trust in the process and tolerance for uncertainty.

Pendulating at the Zero Point

The therapist observes Jenn's internal conflict—her desire to salvage a relationship that is also causing her immense pain. This contradiction highlights the complexity of her experience: love and devastation coexisting, hope and hopelessness intertwined. The therapist remains with this paradox, allowing Jenn to recognise both polarities within her psyche instead of rushing to resolve them.

Critical here is recognising potential introjections—internalised "shoulds" that may not serve Jenn's authentic needs. Voices like "I must forgive" or "I must stay for the children" require exploration. Are these Jenn's true values or inherited expectations that prevent her from accessing her genuine response to the situation?

Simultaneously, the therapist attends to Ben's urgency to "get past it"—his desire for quick restoration of normalcy—while honouring Jenn's need to heal from the shattering of her ground. The therapist pendulates between these positions, neither rushing Jenn toward premature closure nor allowing Ben's anxiety to drive the therapeutic process.

When the therapist states how his needs are not priority, she channels clarity that emerges from this centred position. This intervention arises not from judgement but from attunement to what the field requires in that moment—recognition of Jenn's position as the stable parent while her world collapses.

This positioning at the zero point allows both partners to experience their authentic responses without the therapist's agenda interfering. Ben must face the full weight of his choices, while Jenn can explore her genuine feelings without pressure to forgive or decide. The therapist's creative indifference creates conditions where healing becomes possible, though its timing and form remain unknown.

The following table illustrates key polarities that emerged during Ben and Jenn's session and demonstrates how maintaining creative indifference allowed the therapeutic process to unfold.

A critic might question the therapist's direct intervention—"This is not your moment, Ben"—as unprofessional or overly self-disclosing. Indeed, I have written this moment precisely to highlight this potential controversy and to demonstrate what I recognise sets Gestalt therapy apart from other approaches. While some methods emphasise therapist neutrality or carefully structured responses, Gestalt therapy sees the therapist as a responsive participant in the field, whose genuine reactions offer crucial insights into the relational dynamics involved.

Table 8.1 Polarities and the Therapist's Zero Point in Ben and Jenn's Story

Polarities in the Field	*How They Manifested*	*Therapist's Zero-point Response*	*What Emerged*
Betrayal ↔ Loyalty	Jenn feels her marriage is a lie; Ben wants family restored.	Therapist holds rupture without judgement or premature repair.	Acknowledgement that betrayal cannot be undone, but loyalty to children remains a grounding thread.
Rage ↔ Containment	Jenn restrains her urge to collapse or punish: "a luxury I can't afford."	Therapist validates both rage and restraint, without forcing one.	Jenn's strength and dignity surface alongside her pain, showing she can hold both.
Humiliation ↔ Dignity	Jenn feels exposed and diminished.	Therapist names humiliation without reducing her to victimhood.	Restoration of Jenn's sense of worth and clarity that she is not "the problem."
Fear of Loss ↔ Denial of Consequences	Ben pleads for forgiveness, minimising impact.	Therapist sets boundary: "…not the priority."	Ben begins to face consequences of his actions without shortcuts.
Hope ↔ Hopelessness	Jenn oscillates between salvage and despair.	Therapist pendulates, tolerating paradox without solution.	Permission for Jenn to live her ambivalence without being rushed into decisions.
Blame ↔ Responsibility	Jenn demands "why"; Ben defends.	Therapist redirects responsibility without demonisation.	Ownership shifts back to Ben, allowing Jenn space for her authentic responses.

At this moment, creative indifference demonstrates how it accepts rather than eliminates differences—including the difference between the therapist's embodied response and what traditional therapeutic wisdom might suggest. The therapist experiences a surge of protective anger towards Jenn and frustration with Ben's deflection yet doesn't fall into either pole. Instead, from this centred awareness of opposing forces, a clear response emerges setting a firm boundary that protects the vulnerable partner while holding the other accountable. This isn't permissiveness disguised as acceptance, nor is it punitive judgement. It's the disciplined spontaneity that arises when we stay present with differences— between partners, between ethical positions, and between therapeutic stances—allowing the field itself to reveal what's needed. In Gestalt therapy, we trust that our authentic, centred responses, even when they challenge conventional therapeutic etiquette, serve the deeper truth of the moment. The therapist's ability to feel and respond from the field, rather than from a prescribed position, transforms potential countertransference into therapeutic presence.

Case Study B: Siya and Sam (Part 2)

Several months have passed since we last encountered Siya and Sam in Chapter 5, where their relationship teetered on a precipice. Sam's drinking had escalated, while Siya found herself increasingly unable to maintain the careful management of his behaviour that had characterised their marriage. The "velvet robe" of family expectations and cultural obligation that once gave Sam such privilege had become a weight neither could bear. Now they return to therapy at a crucial moment, a process requiring them to consider the future of their relationship.

Sam's timely arrival at our session sharply contrasts with his prior pattern of absences and excuses. The man who once carried himself with the air of royalty now perches anxiously on the sofa's edge, his usual bravado replaced by something quite the opposite. When Siya enters, still in her courtroom attire, the atmosphere shifts. Sam's demeanour is that of a defendant awaiting judgement.

I notice how differently they occupy space this evening. Siya's certainty fills the room while Sam shrinks away.

"I've been working on myself," he announces first. "My therapist says I should show more appreciation." He fumbles in his sling bag, his movements jerky, and produces a handful of crumpled sticky notes. The paper makes a dry, scratching sound as he smooths them out. "See? I was trying."

He explains how he followed his therapist's suggestion, writing love poetry and gratitude quotes on multi-coloured neon Post-its and placing them throughout their apartment. "To rekindle our love," he adds.

Siya stays composed; a slight twitch at the corner of her mouth betrays deeper emotions. I recognise this look. It is not of anger or sadness, but of tired resignation. She had seen his performance before and had lived through listening to his countless promises and assurances. The long nights spent waiting for him, the sound of his unsteady footsteps in the hallway, but most vividly, the ritual of quietly cleaning his drunken puke from their living room floor so as not to wake their sleeping child.

Siya holds him in place with her unwavering gaze. Sam hunches over. An unfamiliar emptiness weighs heavily on him. His mother's velvet robe is a comfort and a shackle. Is he a deity? A child? Today, however, in the therapy room with his wife, the illusion shatters. Siya refuses to conform to the dynamic shaped by her mother-in-law. No woman of her stature today can accept this role without resentment. She needs him to be, at the very least, a respectful father to her child. He trembles. The unfamiliar weight of adulthood bears down on the fragile walls of a self that feels foreign to him.

"I need you to listen to me, Sam," Siya says, aware of what the written notes and his sudden attention to her mean. "It's not about us anymore. It's about you. There is no us."

"But we have to try," he insists. "For Priya. What do we tell our family?" The crumpled sticky notes lay on the coffee table between us like temple offerings, their bright colours a jarring contrast to the moment's gravity.

She gazes at the coloured tokens of supposed expressions of love, evidence of broken promises she will no longer endure.

"How can you do this?" His voice shrinks to a whisper.

Siya's clenched fists rest in her lap; gold rings glisten around her tightly curled fingers.

There is an overwhelming sense of an ending. I observe their raw honesty emerging. This is likely the most genuine conversation they've had in a session. What remains is an unvarnished, painful, tender truth in a moment of rupture, where there is no pretence, no performance. Their words now carry a quiet intimacy that never existed. It strikes me how love sometimes emerges most clearly in moments of letting go.

"Sometimes," I say, "the truest act of love is the courage to be real."

Sam catches my eye, looking like a child lost.

This is not the time to pick him up. I recognise my impulse to offer some form of consolation, yet I am aware that he, too, has the right to his sorrow.

I stand at a fault line of an impending emotional earthquake. The ground between them trembles with foreshocks. I breathe deliberately and reach for my glass of sparkling water. The ice, sharp and clarifying, mirrored the cold clarity needed in this moment—not detachment, but alert stillness. I'm grateful that I had prepared it before they arrived, as if some part of me had anticipated needing this anchor. The cold sensation on my tongue grounds me.

Their difference is no longer a dance but a chasm. Where once there was movement between them, now there is only space.

"I'm hearing that Priya will still have her parents close by," I say, conscious of meaning to support a direction towards a future shared responsibility. "Some connections must endure even as others dissolve."

"I will never separate my child from her father," Siya assures Sam.

"That's my biggest fear," Sam says, tears freely falling, "to lose time being with my daughter." His mother's velvet robe of devotion, once a source of comfort, now provides none.

"I'm sorry," Sam manages between tears. "Can we still try?"

"Please, Sam, listen to me for once. I am serious." Siya's plea carries the weight of countless unheard requests and years spent managing his moods and cleaning up after him. "This is very hard for me, too."

"Okay," Sam says. "But what will our families think?"

Siya turns to me, opening her mouth but finding no words.

"Let's imagine these voices that we are hearing in this room. What do your mothers say now?" I let the question hang in the air.

"Oh, everyone will have lots to say." Siyas face floods with resignation. "My mother will be hysterical." She straightens her spine as if already bracing for the storm. "Then there is my mother-in-law."

The invisible presence of their families begins to crowd the room: Siya's mother with her concerns about community standing, Sam's mother with her weighted expectations. They are witnesses who have always been integral to their marriage, shaping their choices and limiting their movements.

Siya's voice steadies as she speaks, her words bearing the weight of generations. "Through therapy, I've realised how much the women before me have shaped me. My grandmother, uneducated and powerless, endured a marriage with an unfaithful man. My mother used to tell me about finding her, wailing and helpless, yet unable to leave. My mother was raised to be different, given opportunities my grandmother never had. She built a career, she was strong, but even she accepted neglect from my father, who was absent and resentful as a husband, though a loving father to me." Siya's eyes glisten, the memories vivid and raw. "I see now how much I modelled after them. I can feel it in my bones. I am scolding myself at this moment for making this decision. But I need to stand for myself. I know better now than to pass a legacy down to Priya that will hurt her the way it hurts me now."

"So, I can't stay in this marriage anymore," Siya continues, her voice finding new strength. "I can't forgive myself if I stay."

Siya's words impact me. I nod.

I say to Sam, "This is your chance to do well for your child; she will look to her father to guide her as she grows up."

The words reach him differently now, "I'm not sure," he mutters, speaking to something beyond his loss.

Siya brings her palms together in a gesture that seems both prayer and gratitude, the golden bangles on her wrists catching the light. "Yes, Sam. You have been a loving father, and I can see how you and Priya love each other."

Sam heaves silently, struggling to control more tears; his breath comes in ragged gasps.

"I'm sorry," Siya says, looking first at Sam and then addressing the space in front of them. Her voice carries regret and resolve as she speaks to invisible but powerful presences in the room.

She breathes in deeply and holds that breath, then lets go with an assured sigh.

"And to my mothers, I would say, 'I'm sorry. I need to do this for me and my daughter.'"

The Paradox of Women's Liberation

Siya's reflection on the women who came before her highlights one of modernity's most complex paradoxes. Her grandmother, mother, and her own journey illustrate three generations navigating vastly different social realities—ranging from powerlessness to professional success, from arranged marriages to chosen partnerships, from extended family support to personal autonomy. Yet Siya's freedom to leave an unsatisfactory marriage comes with costs her ancestors never faced. Research consistently shows that women today, despite unprecedented opportunities, report higher rates of anxiety and depression than previous generations (Twenge, 2000; Putnam, 2000). The tribal support systems that sustained women through child-rearing and hardship have largely dissolved. Siya's grandmother, for all her powerlessness, lived surrounded by sisters, aunts, and neighbours who shared childcare, celebrated together, mourned together. Her mother, despite career demands, still had extended family nearby.

Contemporary women enjoy freedoms their ancestors could not imagine, yet often feel profoundly alone in ways earlier generations never experienced. The liberation we've fought for—the right to choose our paths, to leave unhappy marriages, to prioritise our needs—comes with a sense of isolation that would have been unthinkable in more traditional societies. This does not imply that earlier periods were better, but rather that social progress involves compromises that need recognising. As therapists, we see this paradox regularly: clients who have achieved everything feminism promised—education, career, financial independence, reproductive choice—yet they still face loneliness and decision fatigue that their grandmothers, living within clear yet restricting social roles, rarely experienced.

Siya's decision to leave her marriage embodies both triumph and loss: triumph of personal agency over obligation, and loss of the certainty that comes with traditional roles. Her daughter Priya will gain even greater freedom—and possibly even more responsibility for creating meaning and connection in an increasingly interconnected yet fragmented world.

Creative Indifference in Gaps that Cannot be Bridged

Siya and Sam faced unbridgeable differences in their individual needs. One cannot compromise on whether to be married or not. Being at the zero point means experiencing and sitting with the field's emotions, bearing with discomfort that might be and not knowing a way out. Here is where the philosophy serves therapists best. Friedlaender's principles of creative indifference are profound. Looking at Siya and Sam's story above, we can link these principles to the process:

Principle 1: The balanced centre point is a position between polarities that includes both. It is neither neutrality nor indifference to suffering. It is the calm centre where possibilities exist. Being at the centre point is a dynamic stance. When both partners have opposing needs, as with Siya and Sam, creative indifference helps the therapist stay with the phenomenon.

Principle 2: The perception of subjective wholeness. The field lives, breathes, and evolves. Being in the field, the therapist relates to the therapeutic situation as an integrated whole rather than viewing individuals as fragmented parts. There is a suspension of judgement about who's right or wrong, or who's victim or perpetrator, or who's doing more or less. Siya's exhaustion from enduring Sam's behaviour, Sam's terror at losing his marriage, their daughter Priya caught between them, and the invisible presence of the extended family exist as aspects of a single, suffering system. Wholeness is a quality of awareness that allows us to stay with complexity without losing ourselves in judgement.

Principle 3: The freedom from "dividuality" liberates us from evaluating and judging, providing solutions, or fleeing the discomfort. The therapist is encouraged to lean back and consider whenever they feel compelled to console or chide, not to be driven by the professional identity of the helper, the comforter, the teacher, the choreographer, to choose curiosity and presence over action. To be of the field rather than step outside of it.

Principle 4: Creative pathos refers to the vibrant emotional pain within the field that is often ignored or hidden away, yet rich with wisdom. When this suffering is acknowledged openly, it holds the potential for transformation. The therapist's role isn't to erase the pain but to let it come to light. We "stand at a fault line of an impending emotional earthquake." In the stories of Siya and Sam, as well as others in the book, giving suffering a voice allows the creation of possibilities.

Principle 5: A "self-creating" on the therapist's part. There is intentionality in being present. No training manual or supervisor can grant this capacity to be of the field experiencing the pathos.

Principle 6: The integration of opposites. Resolution is not forced. There is no coercion, even though there is pressure for change to happen. Sam's attempts to patch their broken marriage miss the mark, for he had not been present in and aware of the pathos in the relationship. "Sometimes the truest act of love is the courage to be real." As Siya and Sam began to open themselves to the hurt of the situation, they became dialogical and more connected with each other. This contact is the connective tissue.

Principle 7: The living identity or self-actualisation. The clients' fixed roles of abandoned wife and failing husband become more adaptable. Through honest dialogue, Siya and Sam articulate their feelings and thoughts more clearly. Siya begins to move away from her role as the long-suffering wife to become a woman of choice, while Sam embarks on a journey to embody a man unbound by cultural restraints.

Table 8.2 Polarities and the Therapist's Zero Point in Siya and Sam's Story

Polarities in the Field	*How They Manifested*	*Therapist's Zero-point Response*	*What Emerged*
Staying Together ↔ Separating	Sam pleads for family unity; Siya states, "There is no us."	Therapist allows both poles to exist until clarity emerges.	Siya's decision to end the marriage gains clarity, while Sam's grief is honoured.
Performance ↔ Authenticity	Sam offers sticky notes of "love poetry"; Siya rejects performance.	Therapist refrains from shaming or endorsing performance.	Siya is given the space to firmly (and calmly) voice what she feels is true to her.
Obligation to Family ↔ Responsibility to Self	Sam: "What will families think?" Siya: "I need to do this for me and Priya."	Therapist invites imagined family voices into the room.	The larger field (family, culture) becomes visible, and Siya reclaims agency.
Helpless Child ↔ Responsible Adult	Sam trembles, pleads like a child; Siya demands fatherly responsibility.	Therapist resists rescuing, lets both positions be present.	Sam's helplessness is exposed while Siya insists on adult accountability.
Anger/Resentment ↔ Care/Love	Siya's clenched fists vs. her vow not to separate father from child.	Therapist emphasises enduring parent–child bond without pushing reconciliation.	A distinction between marital rupture and parental connection crystallises.
Collapse ↔ Clarity	Sam collapses in grief; Siya voices clear decision to leave.	Therapist validates both collapse and clarity.	The authenticity of an ending is recognised as an act of love and integrity.

The following table illustrates key polarities that emerged during Siya and Sam's session and demonstrates how maintaining creative indifference allowed the therapeutic process to unfold.

The Heart of Creative Indifference

Creative indifference represents a therapeutic stance of recognising polarities while maintaining presence at their turbulent centre. Throughout this book, we've witnessed this philosophy in action across diverse relational challenges. In this chapter, we've explored two of the most intense forms of relational crisis—betrayal and separation—where resolution seems impossible and discord runs deep.

The therapeutic process doesn't advocate for any predetermined outcome, whether reconciliation or divorce. Instead, it honours a deeper truth: while some chasms between partners cannot be bridged, the relationship itself continues to evolve, taking new forms. Creative indifference doesn't seek compromise or resolution as its goal. Rather, by embracing the paradoxical theory of change and remaining fully present within the field, this stance creates space for authentic dialogue.

Through creative indifference, partners can express their truth, communicate their pain, and make genuine contact—even when that contact is difficult and feelings are raw. This approach recognises that while marriages may end, relationships endure, especially when children are involved. The therapeutic work lies in preserving the integrity and dignity of the relationship, regardless of its form. What emerges from this centred stance isn't a solution imposed from outside, but a different order of understanding that arises.

When we started this chapter, the therapy room held its breath as betrayal and separation occupied the space. Now we see that breath-holding differently. Creative indifference isn't passive waiting but active presence—the therapist becoming a still point in the storm, not unmoved by the tempest but unmovable within it. Through Ben and Jenn's shattered trust and Siya and Sam's conscious uncoupling, we've seen how this centred stance creates something revolutionary: space for truth to emerge without dictating its shape.

Conclusion

Having witnessed creative indifference in the situation of Ben and Jenn's betrayal and Siya and Sam's conscious separation, we can now appreciate its deeper philosophical resonance. While Friedlaender arrived at his insights through Western phenomenology, they align remarkably with ancient Eastern wisdom.

In Zen, this is sometimes called the "Middle Way"—not a compromise between extremes but a radical presence that includes both while remaining unbound by either. The Zen notion of "mu" (無)—often translated as nothingness or no-thing—parallels Friedlaender's zero point. This isn't an empty absence but fertile possibility, what Suzuki (1959) describes as "the source of infinite possibilities." When a Zen master holds the teaching stick, ready to strike or not strike, they embody creative indifference—fully present to both possibilities without predetermined action.

Similarly, Buddhist śūnyatā (emptiness) offers another angle on this centred stance. As Nāgārjuna teaches, śūnyatā means the absence of fixed, independent existence—everything arises in relationship, including polarities themselves (Garfield, 1995). From this view, Ben's betrayal and Jenn's loyalty aren't separate phenomena requiring balance but co-arising aspects of their relational field. This alignment with Zen isn't coincidental. Both traditions recognise that transformation comes not from choosing sides but from the still point that encompasses all possibilities. As Dōgen writes in the Genjōkōan, "When one side is illuminated, the other side is dark"—yet the enlightened perspective sees both simultaneously (Tanahashi, 2013). The therapist at the zero point, like the Zen practitioner in meditation, maintains "don't-know mind" (Shrobe, 2004; Suzuki, 1970) —a radical openness that allows the field's wisdom to emerge.

In this chapter, we observe this philosophy reflected through difficult moments in couples therapy. Enduring in this centre involves sitting at a crossroads between ideas of what's right and wrong, feelings of sadness and love, shame, and humiliation.

The zero point also represents time and space. Throughout this book, our couples' therapeutic sessions demonstrate how the present moment in therapy acts as the midpoint between past wounds and future possibilities. Everything that occurs during the therapy session influences the client's perception of the past and shapes their future outcome. The ancient Greeks recognised two forms of time: Chronos (linear, sequential time) and Kairos (opportune time, the moment of possibility, the here and now). When therapists practice creative indifference, they centre themselves in Kairos—the fertile present moment where transformation becomes possible. In Gestalt therapy, our attention is on Kairos, the here-and-now, which anchors our experience in the pivotal moment that is timeless and consequential for the future.

Therapy time feels endless when Sarah and John's decades of separatedness come together through a single shared memory (Chapter 1). The space and moment occupied by an inflated yoga ball sparked contact between Emma and James that had repercussions in their future.

The core idea of creative indifference is to awaken awareness of the infinite centre. By emphasising this centre and recognising its creative potential, it encourages us to sharpen our differences. Honouring differences is the main message of this book. Creative indifference highlights that this is the fertile centre. In Gestalt therapy, we locate this centre at the boundary where contact is made. This contact occurs through the therapeutic dialogue.

This theoretical principle weaves together other fundamental aspects of Gestalt therapy. It reflects Beisser's (1970) paradoxical theory of change in Chapter 3, emphasising change driven by curiosity rather than action. When couples can fully recognise their differences without trying to eliminate them, new possibilities naturally arise. Creative indifferences also align with field theory in Chapter 5 (Parlett, 1991), recognising that polarities and differences are not isolated facts but emergent properties of the entire field, including cultural, historical, and relational dimensions. The phenomenological approach in Chapters 1 and 2 supports creative indifference by suspending interpretation and judgement, allowing differences to be perceived anew without premature categorisation. The spirit of experimentation in Chapter 4 fosters conditions where couples become more aware of how their differences influence their interactions while exploring new ways of engaging with each other.

In our increasingly polarised world, creative indifference offers more than therapeutic technique—it models a way of being with difference that our world desperately needs. When we can stand at the centre between conflicting powers without collapse, we create the "fertile void"—that pregnant emptiness from which new life emerges. Bringing this profound theory to practice is the ultimate gift of Gestalt therapy.

As we prepare to explore integration with other modalities in Chapter 9, we carry this essential question: How do we maintain creative indifference when drawing from different theoretical traditions? Can we stay at the zero point while utilising attachment theory's insights or research-based, manualised interventions?

References

Beisser, A. (1970). The paradoxical theory of change. In J. Fagan & I. L. Shepherd (Eds.), *Gestalt therapy now* (pp. 77–80). Science and Behavior Books.

Frambach, L. (2003). The weighty world of nothingness: Salomo Friedlaender's "creative indifference." In M. S. Lobb & N. Amendt-Lyon (Eds.), *Creative license: The art of Gestalt therapy* (pp. 113–127). Springer.

Friedlaender, S. (1918). *Schöpferische Indifferenz [Creative indifference]*. Ernst Reinhardt Verlag.

Garfield, J. L. (Trans.). (1995). *The fundamental wisdom of the middle way: Nāgārjuna's Mūlamadhyamakakārikā*. Oxford University Press.

Klein, D. C. (1991). The humiliation dynamic: An overview. *Journal of Primary Prevention*, 12(2), 93–121.

Naranjo, C. (1993). *Gestalt therapy: The attitude and practice of an atheoretical experientialism*. Gateways/IDHHB.

Parlett, M. (1991). Reflections on field theory. *British Gestalt Journal*, 1(2), 69–81.

Perls, F., Hefferline, R., & Goodman, P. (1951). *Gestalt therapy: Excitement and growth in the human personality*. Julian Press.

Putnam, R. (2000). *Bowling alone: The collapse and revival of American community*. Simon & Schuster.

Shrobe, R. (2004). *Don't-know mind: The spirit of Korean Zen*. Shambhala Publications.

Suzuki, D. T. (1959). *Zen and Japanese culture*. Princeton University Press.

Suzuki, S. (1970). *Zen mind, beginner's mind: Informal talks on Zen meditation and practice*. Weatherhill.

Tanahashi, K. (Ed.). (2013). *Treasury of the true dharma eye: Zen master Dōgen's Shobo Genzo*. Shambhala.

Twenge, J. (2000). The age of anxiety? Birth cohort change in anxiety and neuroticism, 1952–1993. *Journal of Personality and Social Psychology*, 79(6), 1007–1021.

9 Integration with Other Modalities

Therapist: "Somehow, it's not easy to get things right, is it?"
Claudia: "No, it's not."

— (from Chapter 6)

Introduction: Beyond Theoretical Purity

When Markus demanded, "Just tell us what to do," he voiced what many therapists feel when facing complex couples: the pull toward prescriptive solutions. Yet as we've seen throughout this book, transformation rarely comes from following prescribed techniques. This chapter explores how Gestalt's philosophical foundations can enrich whatever modality you practice, creating space for genuine discovery within structured approaches. This chapter explains Gestalt therapy theory within the framework of the art and science of couples therapy. Theoretical descriptions rarely serve the complex realities of clinical practice. Just as our couples bring multiple cultural influences, personal histories, and relational patterns into the therapy room, contemporary therapists often carry their own uniqueness and diverse theoretical traditions with them. The question we'll ask is how we can integrate meaningfully the ideas of different therapy schools while maintaining philosophical coherence.

In integrating Gestalt with other modalities, therapists may find the approach demanding. It begins with trusting that awareness itself catalyses change, engaging phenomenologically while bracketing assumptions and theories, and staying attuned to the pathos that emerges moment by moment in the field. We are taught to perceive human beings holistically as dynamic fields rather than isolated individuals with separate issues. The experimental stance calls for vulnerability, being willing to accept that outcomes are not for us to pre-empt while trusting the wisdom of the therapeutic process. The most enriching philosophy is in maintaining creative indifference—holding the centre between polarities without agenda or prejudice, being with both the black and the white simultaneously.

While these philosophical commitments challenge therapists to develop new capacities, it doesn't imply that Gestalt therapy exists in isolation. Rather, Gestalt therapy offers a foundational stance—a way of being with

DOI: 10.4324/9781003631545-14

couples—that can inform and enhance work across modalities when applied with philosophical integrity.

Gestalt Principles as Foundation vs. Complete System

Gestalt therapy offers something unique among therapeutic modalities: a philosophical foundation, rather than a collection of techniques or ideas. This distinction is integrative, with the potential to enhance virtually any approach through deepening the therapist's presence and awareness.

Building on the philosophical commitments, we now consider the five core principles mentioned in Gestalt literature (Naranjo, 1993; Perls et al., 1951; Polster & Polster, 1973, Yontef, 1993) and explored throughout this book:

Phenomenology (covered in Chapter 1) doesn't prescribe what therapists should see but how they should notice and feel—with fresh eyes, their five senses and bracketing assumptions. This stance enriches any therapeutic encounter, whether using EFT's attachment focus or Gottman's research-based interventions.

The paradoxical theory of change (covered in Chapter 3) proposes that transformation arises from fully accepting what is rather than trying to be different. This principle does not negate other approaches but can enhance them by encouraging therapists to stay present in the moment, be patient with and trust the process, allowing clients to absorb, process, and internalise their experiences whilst resisting the urge to act on their behalf.

Field theory (covered in Chapter 5) recognises that individual behaviour arises from the entire context of relationships, culture, and history. This perspective is a way of seeing, similar to using a wide-angle lens on a camera, activating the microphone and a magnetometer, thereby expanding any modality's understanding of a couple's life space.

Experimentation (covered in Chapter 4) emphasises discovery through direct experience rather than predetermined outcomes. This attitude can transform rigid techniques, coping skills or "homework" into creative explorations.

Creative indifference (covered in Chapter 8) maintains a centred presence amidst differences. This stance enables therapists to hold multiple perspectives, even therapeutic ideas, without collapsing into narrow thinking or eclecticism.

These principles lie at the heart of therapeutic practice, enriching various approaches to couples' therapy with greater depth and significance, providing a foundation of integration in the work.

Integration with EFT: Attachment and Field Theory

Emotionally focused therapy, developed by Sue Johnson (2019), grounds itself in attachment theory, viewing couple distress through the lens of attachment injuries and insecure bonds. Where Gestalt emphasises the here-and-now field, EFT focuses on attachment patterns rooted in early experience. Yet these perspectives complement rather than contradict each other.

Consider how attachment patterns manifest as field phenomena. For example, when Liam felt "unsafe" as Akina drifted into sleep, his attachment system activated within their current relational field. A Gestalt-informed EFT practitioner might notice not just the attachment trigger but how it emerges in the present moment: Liam's tightening grip, Akina's gradual withdrawal, the atmospheric quality of abandonment filling the room.

The integration becomes practical through phenomenological attention. Rather than immediately categorising Liam's response as "anxious attachment," the therapist first stays with the immediate experience—the word "unsafe" hanging in the air, the visceral quality of his fear. This phenomenological grounding can deepen EFT's attachment focus by ensuring that theoretical understanding doesn't precede genuine contact with the client's experience.

Field theory expands EFT's dyadic focus to include broader influences. Akina's sleepiness wasn't merely an attachment strategy but emerged from a field that included her cram school history, cultural patterns of withdrawal, and the linguistic challenges of therapy in English. By attending to these field conditions, therapists can work with attachment patterns while honouring their complex origins.

The paradoxical theory of change offers EFT something profound: the recognition that secure attachment doesn't come from trying to be securely attached but from fully experiencing one's current attachment reality. When Liam could acknowledge how his father's disappearance echoed in Akina's withdrawal, transformation began not through correcting his attachment style but through deeper awareness of it.

While EFT illuminates how attachment patterns manifest in the field, the Gottman Method brings rigorous research to identifying specific relational behaviours. Here too, Gestalt principles can deepen the therapeutic process.

Integration with Gottman Method: Research, Presence, and Cultural Context

The Gottman Method brings rigorous research to couples therapy, identifying specific behaviours—such as criticism, defensiveness, contempt, and stonewalling—that are said to be predictive of relational outcomes. Gestalt therapy, however, considers all couples as unique phenomena, emphasising emergent processes and present-moment awareness in therapy. This apparent contrast creates a more fertile ground for integration and synthesis.

The Gottman Method (Gottman & Gottman, 2015) defines "masters" of relationships as those who maintain connection despite conflict. Yet what sustains these relationships often involves precisely the kind of attuned presence cultivated in Gestalt therapy. When Sarah finally heard John's tears as he remembered their shared musical rebellion, she demonstrated what the Gottmans describe as "turning toward" a partner's emotional bid. But this turning did not arise from intervention; it emerged through phenomenological presence.

A Gestalt-informed Gottman practitioner might hold research findings lightly, in the background, while keeping immediate phenomenological experience in the foreground. Knowing that criticism is one of the "Four Horsemen" of relational breakdown offers useful context, but recognising how criticism manifests explicitly in a couple's field proves more transformative. Likewise, the Gottmans' "Softened Start-up" technique can be reframed through experimentation: "What happens in your body when you express your need without blame?" Such reframing retains the method's insights while creating space for authentic discovery grounded in the couple's lived process.

The "Four Horsemen" Through a Field-oriented Lens

The Gottman Method identifies four communication patterns—criticism, contempt, defensiveness, and stonewalling—as predictive of relationship dissolution. While this research provides valuable insights, a Gestalt-informed approach invites us to look deeper: What field conditions give rise to these behaviours? What creative adjustments do they represent? How might they serve the organism/environment field, even as they disrupt the relationship?

Contempt: Cultural Context and Protective Distance

When the Gottman Method identifies "contempt" as destructive, we must ask: contempt according to whom? Siya and Sam's relationship breakdown exemplifies the consequences of contempt, brought about by the partner's disdain for the other's behaviour. Mei's withdrawal, almost snubbing of Markus's children, might register as contempt on Western assessment scales, yet in therapy, we discover how it represents appropriate boundary-setting given her history of parentification.

What appears as eye-rolling, dismissiveness, or emotional withdrawal often emerges from specific field conditions. We would consider how contempt might serve as:

- A protective barrier against overwhelming confluence (forced merging)
- A desperate attempt to maintain self when other boundaries have failed
- A culturally shaped expression of disagreement where confrontation is forbidden
- The only available protest against the persistent violation of one's needs

A Gestalt-informed approach reads these behaviours through their meaning within their unique relational field. The therapeutic task is to understand contempt in its context.

Stonewalling: The Body's Wisdom in Withdrawal

What Gottman views as stonewalling, Gestalt therapists recognise as a specific form of retroflection—using muscular tension to hold back a response. The silent partner isn't simply "checking out" but actively containing something. The question becomes: What is being held back?

Most often, it's rage—a protective response to overwhelming field conditions. We see evidence of this across our couples:

- John's careful stillness contained decades of unexpressed longing
- Mei's measured responses held back the scream of the parentified child
- Liam's drinking served as both withdrawal and container for unbearable feelings
- Sam's absences protected both partners from shame

Rather than assuming malicious intent, a Gestalt approach recognises stonewalling as the organism's attempt to accommodate field demands by obliterating differences to secure harmony. The therapeutic work involves:

- Bringing awareness to the muscular holding patterns
- Exploring what's being contained
- Creating safety for gradual expression
- Helping couples recognise stonewalling as an interruption to contact

When partners understand, "When I go silent, I'm protecting us both from my shame," new possibilities emerge for conscious withdrawal that serve the relationship rather than destroying it.

Defensiveness: The Organism Protecting Itself

Defensiveness appears in nearly every couple we've encountered—not as pathology but as the best strategy they've developed to express needs while protecting themselves. From a field perspective, defensiveness often signals:

- Historical experiences where direct expression led to punishment
- Current field conditions where vulnerability feels dangerous
- Unmet needs seeking indirect expression
- The organism's wisdom about what the field can tolerate

Consider Markus's defensive response when the therapist noted his children lived "a 12-hour flight away." His sharp retort—"I go up once every two months to see them"—defended against unbearable grief. The therapeutic response wasn't to break down his defensiveness but to acknowledge the reality with compassion, allowing the grief to emerge naturally.

A Gestalt-oriented therapist becomes curious about the fear behind defensiveness:

- What catastrophe does the person imagine if they spoke directly?
- What historical or cultural field conditions taught them that defence was necessary?
- How does defensiveness serve the relationship system, even as it frustrates direct contact?

Criticism: The Distorted Expression of Need

Criticism pervades troubled relationships, yet from a Gestalt perspective, it represents the organism's attempt to get needs met through the only means it knows. Behind every criticism lies:

- Unmet longing seeking expression
- Anger at repeated disappointment
- Shame about having needs at all
- Cultural patterns where direct requests are seen as selfish

When Siya criticised Sam's drinking, she was expressing multiple layers of need: for a present partner, for safety in her home, for respect of her contributions. When Emma criticised James for always taking the children to his mother's, she was voicing her need to be chosen, to matter, to be part of her own family.

The Gestalt approach doesn't try to eliminate criticism but to:

- Acknowledge the need driving the criticism
- Explore what prevents direct expression
- Experiment with new ways of voicing needs
- Address the field conditions that make criticism feel safer than vulnerability

Transforming the Four Horsemen Through Field Awareness

Rather than viewing these patterns as destructive forces to eliminate, a Gestalt-informed approach sees them as creative adjustments that have outlived their usefulness. This field-oriented understanding transforms the Four Horsemen from predictors of doom into doorways for deeper understanding. When couples can recognise these patterns as creative adjustments rather than character flaws, when they can explore what field conditions call forth these behaviours, transformation becomes possible—not through eliminating these patterns but through developing choiceful awareness about when and how they emerge.

Cultural Context and the Etic/Emic Distinction

Gestalt therapy's field theory allows therapists to situate Gottman-style findings within a broader cultural and relational context. What constitutes "contempt" or "withdrawal" can vary significantly across cultures. For example, Mei's withdrawal from Markus's children might be interpreted as contempt within a Western communication framework. Yet in her cultural context, this behaviour represented a form of respectful boundary-setting. By holding research findings lightly within field awareness, therapists can apply Gottman's insights without imposing universalising assumptions—avoiding the imposition of etic norms onto emic relational contexts.

The distinction between etic and emic perspectives is crucial. Etic approaches rely on externally derived categories and measurements presumed to apply across cultures, such as using the "Four Horsemen" as universal predictors of distress. While these frameworks provide valuable research tools, they risk cultural mis-attunement when applied rigidly. Emic approaches, on the other hand, seek to understand behaviour from within the cultural system itself. What appears as emotional detachment or relational failure in one culture (or in the present field) may, within another, reflect deeply held values of modesty, restraint, protection or respect.

This sensitivity to relational context aligns with Gestalt therapy's emphasis on field phenomena. Instead of pathologising behaviours, the field perspective invites therapists to ask: What relational, familial, or cultural forces are shaping this behaviour in the here-and-now? This question keeps the couple's process at the centre, allowing therapeutic interventions to adapt to what is emerging in the moment—rather than relying on predefined markers of dysfunction.

Integration with IFS: Parts and Field

Internal family systems (IFS) therapy, developed by Richard Schwartz (1995), works with internal "parts" or sub-personalities, while Gestalt therapy traditionally emphasises holistic self-experience as a process rather than an entity. Despite this apparent philosophical divide, both approaches share a fundamental recognition: what appears as individual pathology often represents creative adaptation to difficult circumstances.

Reframing Parts as Fixed Gestalts

From a Gestalt perspective, what IFS calls "parts" can be understood as fixed gestalts—rigid patterns of creative adjustment that have become frozen in time. These aren't literal sub-personalities but organised ways of being that emerge to manage overwhelming field conditions. This reframe transforms how we work with multiplicity in couples therapy.

Consider Ben's relationship with affairs. IFS might identify an "affair-seeking part"protecting him from a vulnerability. A Gestalt lens sees this differently: a fixed pattern emerging at specific field conditions—when intimacy feels dangerous, when he feels unseen, when the marital field resembles his childhood experience of emotional neglect. The question shifts from "What does this part want?" to "What field conditions call forth this pattern?"

Empty Chairs and Parts Work: Different Meanings

Both modalities use empty chair work, but with profoundly different understandings. When Sherlyn placed chairs for her "critical church people," a pure IFS approach might facilitate dialogue between herself and these internal critics. The Gestalt understanding is more radical: those chairs don't hold internal parts but field forces—the accumulated weight of cultural shame, religious prescription, and generations of women monitoring each other's sexuality.

This distinction matters therapeutically. Rather than negotiating with internal parts, Sherlyn was reclaiming her space in the here-and-now from introjects.

When she said "Leave!" she wasn't unburdening parts but overcoming retroflection brought about by the guilt and shame of allowing spontaneous self-expression, which is the essence of intimacy.

Working with Couples' Interlocking Parts/Patterns

Where IFS might explore how partners' parts trigger each other, Gestalt examines how fixed Gestalts interlock to create repetitive patterns of suffering. Emma's "withdrawing part" and James's "absent husband part" aren't separate entities but co-created patterns emerging from their shared field.

A Gestalt-informed IFS practitioner might ask:

- "When this pattern emerges between you, what happens in the space?"
- "Show me with your bodies how these parts/patterns dance together"
- "What field conditions make this the only dance available?"

This shifts focus from internal negotiation to relational choreography.

Trauma and Fragmentation Through Both Lenses

Both approaches recognise trauma's fragmenting impact. IFS sees protective parts forming around wounded exiles. Gestalt sees fixed gestalts—creative adjustments that helped survival but now limit contact. The integration comes in recognising that healing happens not through parts work alone but through new relational experiences with the therapist in the field of the therapy room.

When Liam whispered "I get you" to his absent father, he wasn't unburdening an exile but finishing an interrupted gesture that had kept him confined for years. The therapy room, with the therapist as a compassionate witness, reorganised around this open gestalt, unlocking new possibilities for him.

Creative Indifference and Parts

Perhaps the deepest integration comes through creative indifference. Rather than taking sides with particular parts or trying to strengthen the self, the therapist maintains a centred presence with all manifestations. This doesn't mean validating destructive behaviours but recognising that each pattern once served survival.

The therapist embodies what IFS calls "curiosity and compassion" through phenomenological presence:

- Not "Tell me about your angry part" but "How does anger live in your body right now?"
- Not "Can your Self speak to this part?" but "What happens when you stay present with this feeling?"
- Not "What does this part need?" but "What's happening between you as this pattern emerges?"

The Unity in Multiplicity

Ultimately, both approaches honour the human experience of multiplicity while seeking integration. IFS's "Self-leadership" and Gestalt's "organismic self-regulation" point toward the same wisdom: health comes from fluid responsiveness rather than rigid patterns.

The stories in this book demonstrate this integration. When partners like Ben and Jenn sit with their multiplicity—his conflict between family man and pleasure-seeker, her struggle between dutiful mother and betrayed wife—transformation comes not from parts negotiating but from full contact with their present reality. The field itself holds the wisdom for reorganisation.

A truly integrated approach recognises that whether we speak of parts, patterns, or creative adjustments, we're pointing to the magnificent human capacity to adapt, survive, and ultimately transcend our adaptations through the healing power of authentic relationship.

Conclusion: Beyond the Pursuit of "Healthy" Relationships

Throughout this exploration of integration, we've examined how Gestalt principles can enrich various couples therapy modalities. We've seen how phenomenological attention deepens EFT's attachment focus, how field awareness contextualises Gottman's research findings, and how creative indifference transforms IFS's parts work. These integrations demonstrate the generative possibilities when different approaches meet with mutual respect.

Yet as we conclude, it's essential to acknowledge a fundamental distinction that sets the Gestalt approach apart. While EFT pursues secure attachment, the Gottman Method identifies markers of relationship success, and differentiation-based approaches seek the optimal balance between autonomy and connection, they share a common premise: there exists a standard for what constitutes a "healthy" or "happy" relationship.

This pursuit of relationship health—however well-intentioned—represents a subtle form of diagnosis that pervades contemporary couples therapy. EFT diagnoses insecure attachment patterns to be corrected. Gottman diagnoses destructive communication patterns to be replaced with constructive ones. Even humanistic approaches often carry implicit ideals about what relationships should look like: partners who can self-regulate, communicate effectively, and maintain boundaries while staying connected.

The Gestalt approach presented in this book takes a radically different stance. While we can appreciate and even utilise insights from these modalities, we are not fundamentally concerned with whether a relationship meets criteria for health, success, or optimal functioning. Instead, we attend to the phenomenon of the moment—what is happening between these two people, here and now—and attune ourselves to the pathos of the field.

This distinction returns us to Karl Jaspers' (1923/1963) revolutionary understanding of psychopathology. We recognise that the Greek word "pathos" means suffering or passion, while "logos" means study or understanding.

Thus, psychopathology is not the study of mental illness but the study of the suffering of the soul. For Jaspers, the therapeutic task was to understand human suffering from within, through phenomenological engagement rather than diagnostic categorisation.

In Gestalt couples therapy, we extend this insight: our work involves studying the pathos of the relational field. This pathos—the essential suffering that emerges between people—cannot be diagnosed as healthy or unhealthy, secure or insecure, differentiated or enmeshed. It simply is, in all its complexity and contradiction.

Reflect on how this shifts our perspective on integration. When Siya talks about cleaning Sam's vomit from their living room floor, we could observe attachment patterns (EFT) or contemptuous behaviours (Gottman), but ultimately, we remain attentive to the pathos—the emotional suffering of a woman torn between cultural obligation and personal dignity. When Mei states, "I am not their mother," we might identify differentiation processes or parts establishing boundaries, yet our focus stays on the pathos of a woman reclaiming herself after years of parentification.

This phenomenological stance doesn't mean we lack ethical grounding or ignore harmful dynamics. Rather, it means we trust that by staying radically present to what is—including violence, betrayal, or profound disconnection—the field itself will reveal what needs attention. The couple's organismic wisdom, when given space to emerge, knows far better than our theoretical frameworks what constitutes their unique path forward.

The invitation of theoretical creative indifference, then, is not to abandon other approaches but to hold them lightly. We can draw from attachment theory without becoming attachment diagnosticians. We can appreciate research findings without measuring couples against predetermined standards. We can explore internal multiplicity without losing sight of the whole person in the present moment.

This is perhaps the deepest integration: recognising that while different modalities offer maps of their founders' relational terrain, the Gestalt approach reminds us that the map is not the territory. The living moment between two people—with all its pathos, complexity, and creative potential—remains more profound than any theory can capture.

As therapists, we're invited to become students of this living moment, bearing witness to the pathos of human connection—the exquisite suffering and possibility that arises whenever two people attempt to be both separate and connect. In this witnessing, held with creative indifference and phenomenological presence, lies the potential for something beyond healthy or unhealthy: the possibility of meeting at the boundary of difference.

References

Gottman, J. M. & Gottman, J. S. (2015). The Gottman method of couples therapy. In D. K. Snyder & J. Lebow (Eds.), *Clinical handbook of couple therapy* (5th ed., pp. 129–157). Guilford Press.

Jaspers, K. (1923/1963). *General psychopathology* (J. Hoenig & M. W. Hamilton, Trans.). University of Chicago Press.
Johnson, S. M. (2019). *Attachment theory in practice: Emotionally focused therapy (EFT) with individuals, couples, and families.* Guilford Press.
Naranjo, C. (1993). *Gestalt therapy: The attitude and practice of an atheoretical experientialism.* Gateways/Arica Institute.
Perls, F., Hefferline, R. F., & Goodman, P. (1951). *Gestalt therapy: Excitement and growth in the human personality.* Julian Press.
Polster, E. & Polster, M. (1973). *Gestalt therapy integrated: Contours of theory and practice.* Brunner/Mazel.
Schwartz, R. C. (1995). *Internal family systems therapy.* Guilford Press.
Yontef, G. (1993). *Awareness, dialogue, and process: Essays on Gestalt therapy.* The Gestalt Journal Press.

Conclusion

Beyond the Therapy Room

"And they lived happily ever after."

Introduction: The Wisdom of the Dance

Journeying through the stories of nine couples in this book, witnessing their struggles and transformations, we arrive at a paradox that defines human relationship: we yearn to be loved for who we are, yet being with another challenges our very sense of self. This fundamental paradox echoes Buber's (1923/1958) insight that "all real living is meeting," where the I–Thou encounter—what in Gestalt therapy we call contact between individuals—brings us healing grace, even as it feels threatening to approach. This is because as we near the boundary where we meet, we encounter our differences. Our differences threaten our individual sense of identity, and we fear potential rejection from each other. Moving toward this edge, we encounter the pathos of shame, the emotion that is integral to human relationships, beginning with our very first: the relationship with our mothers.

Ancient wisdom has expressed this understanding in many ways. For Buber, "In the beginning is the relationship." We are born into relationship. The relationship is the field. Hence we are of the field, never separate from it. Our suffering is the suffering of the field; the suffering of the field is our pathology. Christianity's declaration from John that "in the beginning was the Word" is also about relationship, for words connect—particularly words that reflect one's lived experience of the co-created field. This expression is what works in Gestalt therapy: we therapists become part of the couple's field and support the expression of the field's pathos. This brings relationships to life, drawing the individuals in the couple close to the boundary that connects them. In this process there is fear and shame, because that is where these emotions reside. As therapists, our presence in the field supports this process of connection, which in Chapter 7 we describe as the flow between separation, contact, and intimacy.

The stories in this book are crafted to illuminate this process. Sarah and John rediscover connection through decades-old music; Liam connects with

DOI: 10.4324/9781003631545-15

his absent father; Emma and James find each other through a non-verbal interaction as a simple ball rolls across the carpet. These stories show how unique couples can be, sounding almost like fiction, yet they carry a familiar quality that resonates with us all.

What began as an exploration of Resnick and Resnick's (2020) take on Gestalt couples therapy has revealed something larger: a way of understanding human relationship itself. The principles we have examined—staying present with what is, trusting the wisdom of the field, and maintaining creative indifference between polarities—address not only troubled marriages but the fundamental challenge of being human.

In our current era of rapid technological advancement and questions about artificial intelligence, this understanding of human connection becomes even more invaluable. Perhaps this deeper comprehension of how we relate to one another will help us recognise what makes human connection irreplaceable and put to rest any doubts about our essential value as relational beings.

Happily Ever After: When Cinderella Enters Therapy

Of all the moments shared in these pages, one image haunts me: eight-year-old Sarah, standing with her neatly packed bag, sent away while her brother stayed. "I was Cinderella," she said with that wry smile. "I learned to be useful. Very, very useful."

But here's what fairy tales never tell us: what happens after "happily ever after?" When Cinderella wakes up in the palace, does her emotional muscle memory flood her with guilt, seeing others scrub floors? When being chosen doesn't erase a lifetime of servitude? The story ends precisely where real life—and real struggle—begins.

This is where our couples found themselves—in the messy reality after their own fairy tale beginnings. Each discovered what Cinderella would learn: that being chosen doesn't cure the wounds of not being chosen. That love alone cannot overcome patterns carved by survival. They also discovered what fairy tales never imagine: that differences can connect rather than divide. When partners stop trying to rescue or be rescued—when they can acknowledge painful truths without rushing to fix them—new possibilities emerge.

Bringing the Couples Together: A Map of Difference and Change

We've journeyed alongside nine couples, witnessing their struggles and transformations. Now, as we gather their stories together, patterns emerge that illuminate the deeper architecture of relationship—how we get stuck, how we defend against connection, and most importantly, how genuine meeting becomes possible when we stop trying to eliminate our differences.

The table below maps each couple's journey from presenting complaint through hidden patterns to transformation.

Table 10.1 Bringing the Couples Together: A Map of Difference and Change

Couple	*Chapter*	*Presenting Struggle*	*Hidden Pattern*	*Therapeutic Focus*	*Key Transformation*
Sarah & John	1	"So many things wrong"; walking on eggshells for decades	Childhood abandonment (Sarah sent away at 8); both lost in caretaking roles	Phenomenological witnessing; staying with immediate experience	Shared memory of forbidden teenage music bridges decades of isolation
Liam & Akina	2	His drinking to escape; her falling asleep during conflicts	Father's disappearance echoes in her withdrawal; cram school exhaustion patterns	Recognising trauma as creative adjustment in the present	"I get you. I get me" — compassion replaces reactivity
Mei & Markus	3	"We aren't communicating"; pressure to mother his children	Her lifetime of parentification; his unacknowledged grief (children 12-hour flight away)	Paradoxical theory of change; resisting quick fixes	"I am not their mother"—boundaries create space for authentic connection
Sherlyn & Derrick	3	Three years married without physical intimacy	Invisible audiences of family/church crowding private moments	Making phantom presences tangible through empty chairs	"Leave!"– reclaiming intimate space from internalised watchers
Hai & David	4	Gatekeeping vs. paralysis patterns; intellectual connection masks distance	Both carrying loneliness; shame of being seen yet needing to be seen	Role reversal experiment accessing body wisdom	"I felt seen when you took my seat"—empathy through embodiment
Emma & James	4	Living parallel lives; "nobody's home" in their shared space	Childhood invisibility recreated; fear of mattering ("I'm redundant")	Wordless ball exchange bypassing verbal defences	Creating "home" through small acts of presence
Siya & Sam (part 1)	5	His drinking, her exhaustion; the "velvet robe" of family expectations	Cultural field forces; mother's devotion suffocating both partners	Field awareness; sensing the pathos of cultural patterns	Recognising how generational patterns shape present suffering

(*Continued*)

Table 10.1 (Continued)

Couple	*Chapter*	*Presenting Struggle*	*Hidden Pattern*	*Therapeutic Focus*	*Key Transformation*
Liza & Claudia	6	Forced to hide relationship; "I'm disappearing"	Layers of cultural shame; betraying either family or authentic self	Shared somatic experience of shame in the therapy room	Shame transforms from isolation to solidarity through witnessing
Siya & Sam (part 2)	8	Moving toward separation; he wants to save marriage	Misaligned needs; unable to hear each other across roles	Creative indifference; therapist holding polarities	Conscious uncoupling with dignity; breaking patterns for daughter
Ben & Jenn	8	Ten years of hidden affairs revealed; "all a lie"	Humiliation vs. flight from consequences	Creative indifference; establishing necessary boundaries	"You are not the priority"—creating safety for genuine reckoning
Cinderella & Prince	Conclusion	Palace luxury triggers servitude guilt; love isn't enough	Lifetime of usefulness vs. worthiness; rescue fantasies meet reality	Staying curious about differences rather than fixing	Being chosen doesn't cure not being chosen; differences connect

On Cultural Introjects: When Inherited Wisdom Becomes Contemporary Struggle

Throughout these stories, we witness how cultural introjects—beliefs swallowed whole from family and society—create profound relational struggles. These aren't personal failings but collisions between inherited wisdom and contemporary reality.

When Mei declares, "I am not their mother," she differentiates herself from generations of women in her family who extended maternal care to siblings. This cultural expectation, adaptive in extended family systems, becomes what Resnick (2017) calls a "pollutant"—a resource out of place—in her modern partnership with Markus.

Siya's struggle with the "velvet robe" of family expectations represents one way traditional values can create contemporary conflict. However, we might equally encounter families where these same traditions provide strength and resilience, or where modern couples successfully integrate traditional and contemporary values. The therapeutic focus remains on how these particular dynamics serve or constrain this specific couple, not on evaluating cultural practices themselves.

Sam's relationship with his mother reflects a particular family system where emotional boundaries became unclear. This dynamic—where a parent relies on a child for emotional regulation —occurs across all cultures, though it may be expressed differently based on cultural resources and constraints.

Even couples from similar cultural backgrounds face this challenge. Sarah and John, both English-educated Singaporeans, still have different generational expectations. Liza and Claudia have to contend not just with family shame but also the clash between ideals and family values.

These cultural forces are the field that defines the couples. Our therapeutic task isn't to help clients reject their cultural heritage but to support awareness and facilitate conscious choice— to keep what serves while releasing what constrains.

Throughout these chapters, the Gestalt principle—that difference creates the boundary where contact happens—reveals its revolutionary promise. What initially seems to divide us becomes, when truly witnessed, the foundation of genuine meeting. This cites Beisser's (1970) paradox, offering both sobering realism (our patterns run deep, cultural forces constrain us, shame organises entire fields) and radical hope (transformation comes not from eliminating these influences but from fully experiencing them).

A Note on the Nature of These Stories

Before we begin, I must admit: the therapeutic encounters you'll find in these pages are both real and not entirely so. They reflect genuine struggles and authentic transformations, yet they have been shaped by the needs of teaching and the limits of storytelling.

When it comes to real-life therapy, the process is far more complex than these stories imply. Couples attend multiple sessions, each one a distinct episode in an evolving story. Progress is rarely straightforward—it can be chaotic at times. Sessions can be uneventful, filled with long silences that try everyone's patience. They can erupt in tears or laughter, swing between despair and hope, hold moments of intense grief or unexpected celebration. As therapists, we never know what will emerge. We can't plan or predict what will happen.

Most importantly, we therapists are never as composed, insightful, or secure as the narrator in these stories might appear. We work with our clients, and often during that process, we stumble. We tread on toes. We lose our footing. We feel overwhelmed by the field's intensity, confused by contradictions, unsure about how to proceed. Sometimes we say the wrong thing, miss crucial cues, or get caught up in our own reactions. This is precisely why Gestalt therapy principles are so invaluable. They don't give us a script to follow or techniques to master. Instead, they provide a process—a way of being with couples that trusts in what emerges. When we feel lost, we return to phenomenological attention: What am I sensing right now? When we're tempted to fix or rescue, we remember the paradoxical theory of change: transformation comes from accepting what is. When overwhelmed by competing needs, we seek the zero point of creative indifference.

Our work is about the process, not perfect interventions or brilliant insights. It's about being present with what unfolds, including our own imperfections. As I've condensed years of work into these teaching stories, I've clarified what was unclear and given voice to insights that often come later. But behind each polished narrative are countless moments of uncertainty, failed experiments, and mutual confusion.

What remains true in both the stories and real practice is this: when we trust the process—when we stay curious rather than certain, present rather than perfect—the field itself shows us the way forward. The couples in these pages found their paths not because their therapist had all the answers, but because they stayed with the questions long enough for something new to emerge.

The Human Experience: Shame

What makes us irreducibly human is our capacity to experience shame and transform it through witnessing. When Cinderella admits she still feels like a servant, when the prince acknowledges his helplessness to fix her pain, shame is in the air. In this mutual recognition, something sacred occurs—not the dissolution of difference, but genuine connection through shared vulnerability. Shame defines the human condition. This emotion exists only in relationships, arising when we sense our connection is hurt, bent, or broken. It echoes in the abandoned child's scream, throbs in the broken heart, trembles in guilty terror, aches in the lost inner child. This is why intimacy feels treacherous—it invariably awakens shame. In the therapeutic field, the therapist becomes part of the couple's relational field, experiencing the shame that saturates it.

This suffering—what we call pathos—emerges when we attune to the field's atmosphere. Such attunement becomes a masterclass in witnessing, embodying how Karl Jaspers (1923/1963) explains psychopathology, by not diagnosing ailments, but studying the soul's suffering.

Throughout this book, shame surfaces from background to foreground in profound ways. With Sarah and John, shame drives John's exhausting efforts to help and Sarah's inability to receive care—"Feeling cared for is foreign to me." For Liam and Akina, childhood shame echoes in their present: his abandoned child's terror when she sleeps, her exhausted rebellion against impossible academic demands. Mei and Markus carry shame about vulnerability—his grief over lost children hidden behind demands, her boundary-setting emerging from years of forced caretaking. Emma and James embody the shame of invisibility—"I'm redundant, deselected, not chosen"—each retreating to avoid the pain of not mattering. With Liza and Claudia, shame becomes viscerally embodied as all three press fingernails into forearms, transforming self-hatred into shared recognition.

Although AI can analyse conversational patterns and simulate empathetic responses, it lacks the neurobiological architecture required for experiencing shame. As neuroscientist Antonio Damasio (2003) explains in *Looking for Spinoza*, shame emerges from the complex interplay between our limbic system—particularly the amygdala and anterior cingulate cortex—and our embodied consciousness. Panksepp (1998) identifies shame as part of our mammalian emotional systems, rooted in subcortical structures that generate the visceral, whole-body experience of social disconnection. This embodied knowing—what Schore (2003) calls "right brain to right brain communication"—operates through implicit relational knowing, transmitted via tone, posture, and micro-expressions processed milliseconds before conscious awareness. The therapist's ability to feel shame alongside the couple—experiencing that tightening in the chest, the urge to look away—creates what Siegel (2012) terms "interpersonal neurobiology," where nervous systems co-regulate through embodied presence. This somatic resonance, grounded in our evolved mammalian capacity for attachment and social pain, precisely distinguishes human therapeutic presence from algorithmic pattern recognition.

Put simply, the AI cannot feel the weight of shame in the room. It cannot experience the somatic resonance that arises from connections—such as the therapist's chest tightening alongside Sherlyn and Derrick's shared discomfort, or the holding of breath when Siya describes her child's concern for her. The AI cannot suffer shame with us. This embodied knowing—our capacity to wound and witness wounding—defines our humanity. Shame, that most painful emotion, paradoxically connects us through shared recognition rather than elimination. When we sit together where shame resides, feeling its weight without rushing to fix or run, transformation becomes possible. The therapist's ability to feel shame alongside the couple—being "of the field" rather than observing from outside—creates conditions where shame shifts from being an isolating force to a connective tissue.

When we sit together with shame, feeling its weight without trying to fix or escape, we find what fairy tales never reveal: that transformation comes not from being rescued, but from being truly seen.

Conclusion: The Revolutionary Act of Meeting

As I write these final words, I am aware of you, the reader, breathing on the other side of these pages. Between us stretches the same paradoxical space that defines all human connection—we are irreducibly separate, yet in this moment of shared attention, profoundly together. This is the ultimate teaching of the couples whose stories fill these pages: that the capacity to hold both separation and connection simultaneously is not merely a therapeutic skill but the essence of what makes us human.

What we have explored together represents nothing less than a revolution in how we understand relationships. Not the loud revolution of manifestos and movements, but the quiet revolution that happens when two people dare to meet at the boundary of their differences. In an age that promises connection through technology while delivering unprecedented isolation, in a time when couples seek fusion through dating algorithms while marriages decline, we offer something deceptively simple yet profoundly radical: the possibility that difference itself, and the shame that comes with it, is the connective tissue of love. This isn't an easy idea to accept. It requires us to let go of the hope of discovering someone who "completes" us—someone who removes our loneliness or makes relationship easy. It invites us into the beautiful discomfort of authentic connection—where your difference challenges my beliefs, my needs conflict with yours, and our disparities produce the friction needed to ignite contact.

Throughout these chapters, we have witnessed how Gestalt principles (Perls et al., 1951)—phenomenology, the paradoxical theory of change, field theory, experimentation, and creative indifference—facilitate change. And I shall re-emphasise this: these are not therapeutic tools in a kit to collect, but a philosophy of being a therapist. The therapist who sits at the zero point between polarities, who can feel into the field's pathos as their own, who trusts the wisdom of what emerges, offers the revolutionary act of presence no training manual can teach.

For those of us who sit with couples in their most vulnerable moments, we carry a responsibility to sit with the uncomfortable impasse. This impasse, where authenticity inevitably leads us, is that critical juncture where illusions dissolve and raw truth emerges. Like birth itself, once labour begins, there is no returning to the womb. The relationship must move forward into form. Going back is no longer possible; the old patterns have been exposed and interrupted. In this trembling space between what was and what might be, we contain. We resist the urge to rescue, to smooth over, to provide premature solutions. We breathe with our clients as they face that fertile void, where "the nothingness lies that gives birth to worlds" (Chew-Helbig, 2022; Frambach 2003). And this is not a burden—it is a privilege. To witness the moment when shame is transcended and the couple moves towards contact.

As we close this exploration, let us acknowledge what remains open. The couples whose stories we've shared continue their journeys beyond these pages. Sarah and John still navigate the delicate rhythm of contact and withdrawal. Siya raises her daughter with newfound clarity about the legacy she wants to leave. Ben and Jenn face the long road of rebuilding—or consciously ending—what betrayal shattered. Our stories have no neat endings because life is a process, not an outcome. The dance continues, each day bringing new challenges to remain present with what is rather than escaping into what we think should be.

And what of Cinderella and her prince? Perhaps they realise that the true magic was never the transformation from servant to princess, but in being seen and loved.

To you who have journeyed through these pages, who have felt your own relationships reflected in these stories, who have perhaps recognised your own dance of difference—I offer this final invitation. Risk being seen. Dare to see. Trust that in the space between you and another lies not emptiness but possibility. Know that your struggles with difference are not signs of relationship failure but the very ground out of which love sprouts.

The therapy room where I sit with couples is, ultimately, just a room. Four walls, some chairs, the hum of air conditioning. But in that ordinary space, extraordinary moments happen. Two people risk showing up as they are. They stop trying to become what they're not. They cease attempting to change each other into more comfortable versions. And in that release, in that radical acceptance of what is, they discover what we've been exploring all along: they flow, not towards some perfect fusion, but through the natural rhythm of connection and separation, contact and withdrawal, difference and meeting.

The clock has struck midnight.

Dawn breaks on something messy, difficult and real.

The music starts.

The dance begins.

Will you join?

References

Beisser, A. (1970). The paradoxical theory of change. In J. Fagan & I. L. Shepherd (Eds.), *Gestalt therapy now* (pp. 77–80). Science and Behavior Books.

Buber, M. (1923/1958). *I and thou* (R. G. Smith, Trans.). Charles Scribner's Sons.

Chew-Helbig, N. (2022). Understanding Salomo Friedlaender's creative indifference: A psychotherapy case study. *Geštalt Zbornik*, 9, 5–15.

Damasio, A. (2003). *Looking for Spinoza: Joy, sorrow, and the feeling brain.* Harcourt.

Frambach, L. (2003). The weighty world of nothingness: Salomo Friedlaender's "creative indifference." In M. S. Lobb & N. Amendt-Lyon (Eds.), *Creative license: The art of Gestalt therapy* (pp. 113–127). Springer.

Jaspers, K. (1923/1963). *General psychopathology* (J. Hoenig & M. W. Hamilton, Trans.). University of Chicago Press.

Panksepp, J. (1998). *Affective neuroscience: The foundations of human and animal emotions.* Oxford University Press.

Perls, F., Hefferline, R. F., & Goodman, P. (1951). *Gestalt therapy: Excitement and growth in the human personality.* Julian Press.

Resnick, R. F. & Resnick, R. W. (2020, September 7). *From fusion to connection model of relationship [Video].* YouTube. https://www.youtube.com/watch?v=TslbJCA4yuE

Resnick, R. W. (2017). *Introduction to Gestalt therapy [Video].* YouTube. https://www.youtube.com/watch?v=gXG8DOtmmlk

Schore, A. N. (2003). *Affect regulation and the repair of the self.* Norton.

Siegel, D. J. (2012). *The developing mind: How relationships and the brain interact to shape who we are* (2nd ed.). Guilford Press.

Glossary of Terms by Chapter of First Appearance

Chapter 1: First Contact: The Phenomenological Encounter

Atmosphere/atmospheric qualities The palpable emotional climate or "feeling tone" in a therapeutic space. *See also: Field phenomena (chapter 5), Pathos of the field (chapter 6)*

Bracketing (epoché) From phenomenology; temporarily setting aside assumptions and theoretical frameworks to perceive experience freshly. *See also: Phenomenological witnessing (this chapter)*

Here-and-now experience The immediate reality unfolding between people in the present moment. *See also: Contemporaneity (chapter 5)*

Phenomenological witnessing/attention Observing immediate experience without interpretation or judgement. *See also: Bracketing (this chapter), Being "of the field" (chapter 5)*

Pre-reflexive awareness Immediate bodily knowing before language or categorisation intervenes. The bodily sense that arises before our minds label or interpret. *See also: Embodied knowing (chapter 4)*

Chapter 2: Trauma in the Relational Field

Creative adjustment How organisms adapt to difficult circumstances; survival strategies that may outlive their usefulness. *See also: Fixed gestalts (chapter 9)*

Organism/environment field The inseparable unity of person and environment; we are "of the field" not "in the field." *See also: Field (chapter 5), Life-space (chapter 5)*

The third What emerges between therapist and clients; a co-created field with its own emergent properties. *See also: Field phenomena (chapter 5)*

Chapter 3: The Paradoxical Theory of Change in Couples Work

Introjection/introjects Swallowing whole the values/beliefs of others without digestion/integration. *See also: Contact interruptions (chapter 7)*

Paradoxical theory of change Beisser's principle that transformation occurs through fully accepting what is, not through trying to be different. *See also: Organismic self-regulation (chapter 9)*

Chapter 4: The Transformative Role of Experiments in Gestalt Couples Therapy

Embodied knowing/awareness Understanding that comes through bodily sensation rather than intellectual comprehension. *See also: Pre-reflexive awareness (chapter 1)*

Experiments Investigative exercises conducted during therapy

Figure and ground (die Grund) Gestalt concept where "figure" is what emerges into awareness from the "ground" (background/foundation of experience). *See also: Figure sharpening*

Figure sharpening To bring underlying needs, sensations and emotions to the surface in a therapeutic encounter

Safe emergency Paradoxical state where enough anxiety mobilizes change within safe boundaries

Suppressive vs. expressive techniques (Naranjo) Suppressive: interrupts habitual patterns; expressive: invites hidden aspects into awareness. *See also: Experiments*

Chapter 5: Field Theory in Couples Therapy

Aesthetic sensing/dimension The felt, atmospheric quality of experience; perceiving through resonance rather than analysis. *See also: Embodied knowing (chapter 4)*

Being "of the field" Therapist as participant in the therapeutic situation, not external observer. *See also: Phenomenological witnessing (chapter 1)*

Changing process Field theory principle; fields are dynamic, constantly reorganising

Contemporaneity Field theory principle; how past and future collapse into the present moment. *See also: Here-and-now experience (chapter 1)*

Field/field theory The totality of coexisting facts conceived as mutually interdependent (Lewin). *See also: Organism/environment field (chapter 2), Life-space (this chapter)*

Field forces Invisible influences (cultural, historical, relational) that shape behaviour and experience. *See also: Organisation (this chapter)*

Field phenomena Experiences that emerge from the entire relational context rather than individual minds. *See also: The third (chapter 2), Atmosphere (chapter 1)*

Life-space Lewin's term for the totality of a person's psychological environment (person + environment). *See also: Field (this chapter)*

Organisation Field theory principle; how all elements in a field relate to and influence each other. *See also: Field forces (this chapter)*

Possible relevance Field theory principle; everything in the field potentially matters

Singularity Field theory principle; each field configuration is unique and irreplaceable

Chapter 6: Shame, the Pathos of the Field

Pathos/pathos of the field The essential suffering or emotional quality that permeates a relational space. *See also: Field phenomena, Atmosphere*

Response-ability The capacity to respond flexibly rather than react from habitual patterns. *See also: Creative adjustment (chapter 2)*

Retroflection Turning back on oneself what one wants to do to/with others. *See also: Contact interruptions (chapter 7)*

Chapter 7: The Cycle of Connection: Movement Between Contact and Withdrawal

Confluence Temporary healthy merging where boundaries become permeable. Different from fusion which is permanent

Connection model Alternative to fusion; honors two separate individuals who choose to dance together

Contact boundary The edge where two people meet while maintaining their separateness. *See also: Contact vs. connection (this chapter)*

Contact vs. connection Contact: specific moments of meeting at the boundary; connection: the entire dance/flow between phases

Contact interruptions Patterns that prevent genuine meeting between people. *See also: Retroflection (chapter 6), Introjection (chapter 3)*

Fusion model Traditional view where "two become one" in marriage. *See also: Connection model (this chapter)*

Isolation Protective withdrawal with barriers; different from healthy solitude or withdrawal

Chapter 8: Creative Indifference: Conflict and the Therapist's Centred Presence

Chronos vs. Kairos Chronos: linear, sequential time; Kairos: opportune/meaningful time, the fertile present moment

Creative indifference (Schöpferische Indifferenz) Friedlaender's concept of maintaining a centred position between opposing forces without bias. *See also: Zero-point (this chapter), Fertile void (this chapter)*

Dividuality The state of being divided or experiencing oneself as split; opposite of individual wholeness

Fertile void The creative emptiness where new possibilities emerge. *See also: Zero-point (this chapter), Mu (additional terms)*

Schöpferisch vs. Kreativ German distinction: Schöpferisch (divine creation from nothing) vs. Kreativ (artistic rearrangement)

Zero-point The centred position between polarities; the balance point. *See also: Creative indifference (this chapter)*

Chapter 9: Integration with Other Modalities

Emic vs. etic perspectives Emic: understanding behaviour from within a cultural system; etic: applying external/universal categories across cultures

Fixed gestalts Rigid patterns of being that emerged as creative adjustments but became frozen. *See also: Creative adjustment (chapter 2)*

Organismic self-regulation The organism's natural wisdom to move toward health when unimpeded. *See also: Paradoxical theory of change (chapter 3)*

Theoretical creative indifference Maintaining a centred position that draws from multiple approaches without collapsing into any single framework. *See also: Creative indifference (chapter 8)*

Additional Cross-cultural/Philosophical Terms

I-thou encounter (Buber) Genuine meeting between persons where each is fully present.
Śūnyatā Buddhist concept of emptiness/interconnectedness. *See also: Fertile void*
Mu (無) Zen concept of nothingness/infinite potential. *See also: Fertile void (chapter 8), Zero-point (chapter 8)*

Index

For Product Safety Concerns and Information please contact our EU representative GPSR@taylorandfrancis.com Taylor & Francis Verlag GmbH, Kaufingerstraße 24, 80331 München, Germany